FIRST EDITION

THE REALTOR'S MAGIC FORMULA

ROB VIVIAN

Something awesome is going to happen today!

The Realtor's Magic Formula

ISBN: 978-1-987857-89-4

Typeset and cover design by Edge of Water Designs, edgeofwater.com

Printed in Canada

9 8 7 6 5 4 3 2 1

This book is also available in bulk.

INTRODUCTION

THIS BOOK IS a step-by-step guide explaining and laying out a simple path for any Realtor to follow to attain the desired level of success that is correct for them. This book is very much a how-to with an emphasis on structures and procedures. I'm making the assumption that your brain is in the right place and that what you are thinking is correct, which might be a bit of a stretch for most people. Although the structures and procedures discussed and explained are rock solid, nothing overrides you to become what you think about. So, before jumping into the exact plan for the ultimate Real Estate career, let's visit our brain and see what's going on in there.

At the end of the day, whatever you believe about your Real Estate career will ultimately play out. The future Realtor you become will simply be an echo of your current thinking about your ability, what you feel you can accomplish, and what you personally believe you deserve.

If you have been selling for a while you know that every time you are heading for vacation the phone rings off the hook starting seventy-two hours before you leave. Perhaps you are taking off to the Caribbean on Saturday, and on Wednesday you get a call from someone informing you that it's time to get their home on the market. You say, "Wow, that's great." However, what you're thinking is, *You've got to be kidding me—you have been on the fence for six months and now you want to sell.* The next day another call—"We're ready to look for a property to buy." Again, you say, "Wow, that's great," but you're thinking, *Really, you told me two months ago you were going to wait until spring.*

When I share this in a seminar format, everyone who has been licensed for a while is laughing and the new licensees don't get it. The experienced Realtors say to the new licensees, "Rob's right, that's exactly what happens." The new Realtors inquire, "Well, why does that happen?" The experienced ones respond with, "I have no idea, but Rob's right, that is what happens every time."

I say to the class and to you folks reading this book, "What if I could show you why the phone rings off the hook starting about seventy-two hours before you go on vacation? And what if I could show you how to have that type of energy in your business permanently?" You see, folks, that kind of activity isn't an accident; there is a reason it happens. And if we can understand the principles that create it, then we can duplicate it, thus, making it permanent.

First, let's look at why it happens. Those who are reading this book and have been selling for a while know that this phenomenon doesn't happen just sometimes—it happens every time. When you are heading to the Caribbean on Saturday, or wherever you are going that you are excited about, your subconscious mind travels there on Wednesday, about seventy-two hours prior to you traveling. Seventy-two hours later, your conscious mind catches up when you arrive at your destination. When I explain this to Realtors they often say I am not thinking at all about the trip yet I'm really focused on the business for the next couple of days.

I know right now you are very focused on dealing with the increased opportunities. However, what you need to understand is you are explaining what your conscious mind is thinking. You obviously can't be aware of what your subconscious mind is thinking—if we could, it wouldn't be called our 'subconscious' mind. Although your conscious mind is focused on dealing with wrapping up the business and getting on the plane Saturday morning, your subconscious mind is soaking up rays at the beach sipping on a cool drink.

All the power of your brain resides in the subconscious mind and, when it's in a good state, it brings good things to you. When it's in a bad state, it brings bad things to you. This is *the law of attraction*. Seventy-two hours before you take off for your vacation, your subconscious mind is in a perfect state to attract great things to you. This also means that prior to the seventy-two-hour period, your subconscious mind must have been in a state that was effectively blocking business from coming to you.

The solution would be to either book a vacation for the last week of every month to ensure a lot of business would find you every month, or on purpose put your brain in a state that emulates the state your brain would be in seventy-two hours prior to vacation. Remember that seventy-two hours before you take off on vacation, your brain isn't in the correct mindset; it just emulates that mindset.

There are a few things you can do to be in the proper mindset to attract business:

1) **Be a person that lets things go quickly.**
   Nothing will close you down mentally more than being a person who can't let things go. In life and business, lots of things don't go your way—that's the way it is for everyone. If you are someone who can't let things go, your subconscious will always be in a bad state. It's hard to attract great things into your life when

your subconscious mind is in a bad way. The good news is at least it will be in the right state seventy-two hours prior to your upcoming vacation.

2) **You need to believe in what you are doing.**
This part will be easy—that's what the balance of the book is about: the exact plans to have the Real Estate career that you want. Once you combine these two attributes, you'll have the ability to get over things quickly and an absolute belief that what you're doing is the correct path for you. Then your subconscious brain will be focused on work days and the activity that other Realtors experience seventy-two hours prior to vacation will be permanent for you.

Obviously, the better your mindset, the better this material will work. Although the path we teach is well thought through and is helping thousands of Realtors around North America achieve optimum potential, at the end of the day your success will be dictated by your thinking. You become what you think, and what you think about overrides solid structure.

TABLE OF CONTENTS

Everything you want is
on the other side of fear.

Jack Canfield

ONE

THE MAGIC FORMULA "OVERVIEW"

BEING A REALTOR can be such an awesome job on so many levels. For starters, you have the ability to earn a much higher-than-normal income, an income equal to doctors, lawyers, accountants, and so many other professions that take years of schooling and preparation to be in a position in their trade. I know it's a lot more challenging these days to acquire a Real Estate license; however, in comparison to other professions with equal income potential, preparing yourself to become a professional Realtor is a lot quicker and dramatically less expensive.

Secondly, you have an opportunity to assist others in achieving their goal of home ownership or selling and acquiring their dream home. Maybe they are selling their large home and for the same money purchasing a lake property and a condo. Either way, whatever they are up to, whatever their plan is, you have an opportunity to come alongside and assist them in their amazing venture.

Thirdly, and maybe the most important of the three, is the satisfaction of a job well done. It's that feeling you have when a client takes possession of their new dream home, looks at you and thanks you for making it happen; when they say with sincerity in their heart, "Thank you. We couldn't have done it without you." That right there is the reason most Realtors do what they do. It's the reason we commit so much and take the entrepreneurial risk—to get that handshake and the sincere 'thank you'. That's what makes it all worth it, and that's what drives the majority of Realtors.

I am totally on side with this concept. My job as a Real Estate Coach and Trainer is to assist you in having that amazing feeling more often. When you go home and have someone ask, "How was your day?", your response would be, "I had an amazing day. The Smiths took possession of their new home today. They are really excited and they couldn't thank me enough. I'm very happy for them." I know this also means you will be getting a nice cheque in the next week or so; however, at this point, it feels kind of secondary to that feeling of satisfaction from the Smiths, whose appreciation is outweighing your personal financial gain. Of course, we are in the business to be profitable, and it will be exciting to take that cheque to the bank. I always like the look on the teller's face when they see that larger-than-normal cheque.

This book is about making sure that you go home more often with that awesome feeling of accomplishment, that feeling of doing a good job for someone, and playing your part in the accomplishment of one of their larger life goals. Also, of course, that fun trip to the bank more often. I know lots of you never go to the bank anymore, but the concept is the same either way.

Unfortunately, most Real Estate boards have a failure rate of about 80 percent in the first two years. That means four out of every five Realtors pack it in in the first two years. Obviously they couldn't find a way to help enough people accomplish their Real Estate goals. Unfortunately, when they arrived home and someone asked them how their day was, they were not in a position to say, "Awesome day—the Smiths took possession of their new home and they couldn't thank me enough." Instead, they would say, "Busy, very tiring. I think I'm going to take a nap."

It's funny that when we do it right, everything is amazing, and when we don't do it right, we become frustrated and somewhat cynical. "Hey, how was your day?" And we respond, "Another buyer lied to me." *Buyers are liars.* If you have been selling for a while, you know that's a Realtor saying. We should work towards having more amazing stories of accomplishment and fewer stories complaining about the Buyers and Sellers.

Well, that's where this book comes in—*The Realtor's Magic Formula*, the magic formula to a lot more amazing stories.

When you arrive home and someone asks, "Hey, how was your day?", you respond, "Fantastic day! The Smiths took possession of their new home today and they couldn't thank me enough. What a great day."

"Congrats! Isn't that your fourth closing this month?"

"Yes, yes it is. Life's good."

So, you might be thinking, *Do you really have a magic formula, Rob?* The answer is yes. I do. I have taught this formula to thousands of Realtors, maybe tens of thousands. However, with over three million Realtors in North America alone, it's still somewhat of a secret—at least at the writing of this book. We teach this formula to our coaching clients, then hold them accountable to the principles that make up the formula.

This formula isn't geared to any specific group of Realtors. Our current coaching clients are one-third new at less than one year's experience, one-third one-to-five years' experience, and one-third five-years-plus experience. The program works the same regardless of your experience. Recently, we were hosting one of our larger two-day-events with probably 600 plus in attendance for the two days. I decided on day two that we would have a panel of four of our superstar clients on the stage with me for about thirty minutes so they could tell the audience how they sell thirty to forty homes annually with eight weeks' vacation. Oh, yes, we teach eight weeks' vacation. Being a workaholic is not part of the magic formula.

So, at this particular event, I decided to feature Realtor clients that sold thirty or more homes in their first year as a Realtor. We have an amazing online tracking system for all the clients, so when I asked the staff to filter out all the local clients that sold thirty or more in their first year, that was just a simple few minutes of filtering. They came back with sixty-eight of which I selected four. When I was finished interviewing them from the stage and the audience had asked all their questions, I instructed the panel members to tell the audience how long they have been selling. They all replied, "It's my first year."

I wouldn't say we had a rebellion on our hands, but I will say those present had a hard time accepting that they were being out-produced by some new Realtors. The four panellists on the stage with me were working the magic formula; those in attendance were learning the magic formula. I explained to the audience, "Although these four are truly amazing people, are accomplishing something extraordinary, and are experiencing that unbelievable feeling of accomplishment and personal satisfaction, we did have sixty-eight local Realtors to choose from."

The thing with the magic formula is it's insanely simple. It's so simple that if you've been selling a while, you might wonder why you didn't know this already. You might be surprised that something this simple has managed to elude you your entire career. It's very common; as a matter of fact, it happens almost every day. I'll finish a seminar and someone will come up to me and say, "You know, I have been selling Real Estate for ten years and I did not know that." Then they usually say, "I'm a little surprised that I never noticed that before. They should be teaching this in Real Estate school."

Sometimes, when something is too simple, it's harder to accept when our brain tells us that there must be more to it. In this case, get over the simplicity of the magic formula so you can have more conversations like, "I had a great day. The Smiths took possession of their dream home and they couldn't thank me enough."

The magic formula has three parts. The following chapters all deal with current Real Estate skills and understandings. You will notice that I use and explain a lot of psychology in our skill set, understanding how the brain works, why to say things in a certain way—which words and phrases push clients away, and which draw them to you. After this chapter, it's all about how to be a skilled Realtor; however, don't fool yourself. Without the magic formula you can be as skilled as you want, but it's not going to help you much without the implementation of the magic formula. We teach our clients all the necessary skills required to operate in the highly competitive Real Estate industry, but we hold them accountable to the magic formula. The skills support the magic formula—not the other way around.

IN A NUTSHELL

Let's make sure we have the career we desire and, in turn, help a lot of folks accomplish their goal of home ownership. It's important that we want success for the right reasons. This book will guide you through the process.

You look out there and there are people that their day is changed because of your contribution to it!

Brad Paisley

TWO

The Magic Formula: Step One "The Numbers Game"

THE NUMBERS GAME

WE ALL KNOW that the Real Estate business is a numbers game. I often start a seminar by asking the question, "Who has heard that the Real Estate business is a numbers game?" Everyone puts their hand up. Then I ask, "Okay, someone explain it to me."

They look at me a little confused, and say, "We know it's a numbers game, but we don't know what the numbers game is."

I respond, "Don't you find that a little odd? You know it's a numbers game but you don't know what that numbers game is."

They respond, "Well, we didn't find it odd until right now."

It's honestly kind of funny at first—they have this realization that although they have always known that their personal career path industry is and has always been a numbers game, they really have no idea what it is or how to play it. So, I definitely have their attention when I ask them if they would like to understand the numbers game and how to play it.

The numbers game of Real Estate is that one in four leads work out. For example, this means that this weekend a potential buyer could walk into your open house and you hit it off with them, and they are looking to get into a property as soon as possible. That's a great lead—they might even leave the open house and say to each other, "You know, I really like her. We should use her as our Realtor." I think that happens all the time. Unfortunately, you would not be the only open house they visit that beautiful sunny Sunday afternoon. The next day at their place of work they could casually mention to a colleague that they're looking to purchase a property, and the colleague could ask them if they have a Realtor. Even though they are just one day removed from considering you for the job of finding their perfect dream home, their response to their co-worker is always the same: "We have someone but we're not committed to them." Their colleague could then mention that they have an excellent local Realtor and would be happy to connect them, to which the buyers agree, and there goes your lead.

The truth is that lead had a one-in-four chance of working out for you right from the get go. It's a mistake to view it any differently. It's a mistake on the Realtor's part to put so much stock in that lead. Unfortunately, most Realtors over-invest mentally in each lead, obviously leading to a lot of frustration and stress. A much better plan would be to understand and play the numbers game. If you would like to sell twenty-five homes in any given year, you require 100 leads or, if you want to sell thirty homes, you'll need 120 leads—whatever your goal is, you can do the math. Once you understand and accept this concept, your awesome Real Estate career takes a total different trajectory.

Let's say you are on this plan of making twenty-five sales this year, and it's that beautiful Sunday. In comes this couple into your open house and the three of you hit it off. They leave thinking they really like you and think they should hire you to help them find their perfect home. From your side, you open your journal and record them as a new client found. You track your leads, making sure you find 100 in this calendar year so that your goal of twenty-five sales, twenty-five families successfully moved, will be accomplished. In your journal you have 100 lines for a lead to be recorded. So, you write their name on the next open line. They occupy line forty-three. With a slight smile you think, *I need 100 leads this year to make my sales goal a mathematical absolute. I should have fifty leads by June 30th—the halfway point. It's mid May and I've just found lead number forty-three. I'm on track.*

Nothing will change in the way you view them, treat them, or follow up with them. Everything will be exactly the same, except you will avoid the massive disappointment if this lead doesn't work out. Obviously these newfound clients could be the one in four that work out; however, the more likely scenario is that they'll fall into the three in four that don't work out. I'm explaining absolute mental freedom here—find the appropriate leads, let the chips fall where they fall, hit your goal, and be a happy camper. Find 100 leads, let seventy-five fall away, and be ecstatic that your goal has been achieved. As soon as the buyers leave the open house, Realtor "A"—who is not working on the magic formula—would mentally calculate the commission in their head and begin the process of over-committing on every level: physically, mentally, and emotionally. Obviously, Realtor "A" is destined to be disappointed on a regular basis. On the other hand, Realtor "B" understands and is actively working the magic formula. It's a whole different ball of wax. When the prospective buyer leaves the open house, Realtor "B" records their name on the appropriate line and the entire process is understood and kept in the proper perspective. There are two scenarios: Realtor "A" and Realtor "B". One is frustrating and one is awesome.

The truth is it's a lot easier to focus on leads than on transactions. When a new Realtor asks me if I think they can sell twenty-five homes in their first year, I respond by asking them if they can find 100 leads in a year. For a lot of new Realtors, visualizing selling twenty-five homes in their first year can be intimidating. When asking a new Realtor what is easier between focusing on twenty-five transactions or finding 100 leads, the response is always, "Well, finding 100 leads." Absolutely, of course it is!

There are a couple of interesting things to understand about this numbers game. Both of these items are really good news for the Realtor:

INTERESTING POINT #1

The game of one in four leads working out isn't connected to your years of experience. As previously mentioned, our coaching clients are about one-third newer with one year or less as a Realtor, one-third with one to five years experience, and one-third with five years or more. As we look at all the numbers at the end of every calendar year, we notice that there isn't really any difference between newer Realtors and experienced Realtors, at least in regards to the one in four leads working out.

So, the obvious question would be: why wouldn't a Realtor with more years' experience have a better hit ratio? That's a fair question. After all, one would think that the longer you sell Real Estate, the better you get, and the more you should improve your numbers. The answer is actually the other way around. How is it that a new Realtor can achieve the same numbers as an experienced Realtor? That's really the better question. One in four leads working out are the numbers of an established Realtor. The reason a new Realtor can achieve that skilled number prior to having the skill is that they have a human behaviour characteristic on their side. Human behaviour is a funny thing, and there are lots of behaviour characteristics. In this case, the characteristic that helps the new Realtor achieve the same level as a skilled Realtor in lead conversion is the fact that most people want to give the new person a chance. This translates to buyers and sellers using the new Realtor and feeling good about it. Once you factor in this behavioural characteristic, the new Realtor now has the same lead conversion as the Realtor practising for five years or twenty years.

The only difference would be what the three out of four potential leads are saying. For the new Realtor, I'm sure the story would be something like, the new Realtor is too new, they haven't sold homes in this area, they haven't sold homes in this price range, or maybe they are just simply too young. This will definitely be the flavour of the conversation for a new Realtor. When new Realtors ask me what I say when buyers and sellers ask questions like this, I'm quick to point out that they can't really move the margin. For now they hear these comments, but later, as they progress through their Real Estate career, the comments or objections will change. In the future they will hear, "You are busy and successful, so we want to give someone else a chance." There is no doubt, as time goes by, the story or flavour of the three out of four not working out will change, but the one-in-four game is always the number. This is really great news; at the beginning of every year you know the number of leads required to make your transaction goal a mathematical absolute.

There is a bit of a caveat to the one-in-four numbers game working out. It only applies to fifty-five transactions or less. Fifty-five transactions require 220 leads that are looking to buy or sell within ninety days. Any transaction goal less than fifty-five is one in four. Once you go over fifty-five transactions annually, you start to carry some clout. At that volume, when you start working with new clients, there is a good chance they would already have heard about you and you are one of the top Realtors in your community. For these Realtors, their number can be one in three or maybe even as low as one in two. However, be clear that if your transaction goal is less than fifty-five annually, then your number is one in four.

INTERESTING POINT #2

The other interesting fact about the numbers game of Real Estate is that the market doesn't matter. At the writing of this book, the Greater Toronto Area is engulfed in an all-out extreme seller's market. At the same time, many of our clients in different parts of North America are experiencing different markets. There are five markets for the Realtor to navigate:

1. An extreme Seller's market
2. A moderate Seller's market
3. A neutral market
4. A moderate Buyer's market
5. An extreme Buyer's market

In the Toronto market, 20,000 active listings is considered a normal or neutral market not leaning towards the Seller or the Buyer; 10,000–14,000 active listings is an extreme Seller's market; 14,000–20,000 active listings is a moderate Seller's market, leaning to the Seller. If the current inventory were to exceed 20,000 active listings, it would lean towards the Buyer, 20,000–23,000 a moderate Buyer's market, which means any amount of active listings exceeding 23,000 would be an extreme Buyer's market. Supply and demand drives this principle. You can research your particular board and educate yourself as to what inventory level dictates which of the five markets.

As I mentioned, at the time of writing of this book, the Toronto market is experiencing an all-out extreme Seller's market (10,000 active listings). So, for Toronto Realtors in this market heavily stacked towards the Seller, their numbers game is one-in-four leads working out. If they want to sell twenty-five homes, 100 leads are required. We coach a lot of Realtors around North America, so all five potential market options are covered. Those in Seller's markets have the one-in-four game, those in Buyer's markets have the one-in-four game, and those in neutral markets have the same.

Once a Realtor can grasp and understand this principle, they realize that there really isn't any rough water for them; one in four is the number. I find it interesting that the vast majority of Realtors really do not possess this understanding. I know this because every time in every marketplace when the cycle of the market changes—when a market switches from a Seller's market to a Buyer's market—a large group of Realtors goes out of the business. They see some negativity in the media headlines like "Housing market peaks beginning to correct" and they get nervous and off they go to other career options.

What difference does it really make to the Realtor whether the market remains in a Seller's market or converts to a Buyer's market? If a Realtor has a goal of twenty-five transactions, 100 leads are required whether or not the market remains advantageous to the Seller. Now that the market has changed and transitioned to a Buyer's market, that same Realtor would still require 100 leads to facilitate twenty-five transactions.

Understanding this numbers game changes everything for the Realtor. When I teach this in a seminar format, when I enlighten Realtors to how their business really works, it is common that someone responds, "So there really isn't any rough water in the Real Estate business?"

I respond, "No, that's not true. There's lots of rough water, sometimes *really* rough water, that's difficult to navigate."

Because the Toronto market is currently in an extreme Seller's market, there is very rough water for Buyers because it's very difficult for them to navigate. If the market were to switch to an all-out Buyer's market, then there would be rough water for Sellers. Unless you are in a neutral market—relatively calm water—there is always going to be rough water for somebody, just not the Realtor, because for Realtors, the numbers game is always one in four.

Over time, things tend to balance out. At the end of your Real Estate career you will notice that, along the way, you were in a Seller's market about the same amount of time you were in a Buyer's market. It's nice to know moving forward that, regardless of the market, one in four leads working out is the number to focus on. When the market makes a switch, you will still need to make some adjustments. For example, in an all-out Seller's market, pricing or servicing the listing isn't as important. If the price is a little high it will sell anyway because it's an aggressive Seller's market. Listings sell in the first week so servicing isn't required as much. On the other hand, if you are selling right now in a Seller's market and the market migrates to a Buyer's market, the one-in-four leads required would not change but you would need to brush up on your servicing and pricing dialogues.

IN A NUTSHELL

Moving forward in your career, as the market continually changes, you will need to brush up on some skills that were not as important in the previous market; however, the one-in-four leads working out remains constant. This will be really comforting for you to know as you travel through your Real Estate journey—there will be ups and downs for Buyers and Sellers but not for the Realtor. If you have the desire to sell twenty-five homes in a calendar year, then your required number of leads is 100. During that particular year it could be challenging for Buyers or Sellers, depending on the market, but for you, there will be one in four that will work out.

You don't have to be a mathematician to have a feel for the numbers!

John Forbes Nash Jr.

THREE

THE MAGIC FORMULA: STEP TWO "THREE PILLARS"

WE ALL HAVE heard the saying "we should never put all our eggs in one basket". Of course this is true for many things, including running a Real Estate business. Unfortunately, Realtors are notorious for making this mistake. Realtors tend to migrate to something and then that's the only thing they do. Maybe as a new Realtor, another Realtor mentions that they do well with open houses or a geographical farm is working for them. The new Realtor thinks, *That sounds good, I can do open houses* or *run a geographical farm*, and so off they go, focusing on a geographical farm or specializing in open houses. The problem is the Realtor now has all their eggs in one basket.

Over time, the one item that a Realtor has chosen becomes their Real Estate identity. When other Realtors talk about that Realtor, they connect him or her to that activity. For example, Realtor Sally is a farmer, or Sally specializes in open houses, or maybe Sally only works for sale-by-owner or expired listings. Like all things in life, we need a balanced approach. There are many ways to generate leads although traditionally there are six pro-active sources, or "pillars", for the Realtor to choose from.

PROACTIVE SOURCES: "PILLARS"

1. Working your past clients and centre of influence
2. Geographical farming ("community marketing")
3. For-sale-by-owners ("private sales")
4. Previously listed properties ("expired listings")
5. Open houses
6. Calling around just-listed or just-sold properties

Of course, leads can also come from the Internet, although those don't fit into the previously mentioned one-in-four leads working out. All a Realtor needs to do is select three sources that suit them, with "past clients and centre of influence" as their number one source "Pillar". All six pillars work—all will generate leads. The trick is to select the three that best suit your personality as long as your past clients and centre of influence is the number one pillar. If a Realtor sets a goal for twenty-five transactions in a year, then by now you know that 100 leads would be required for one in four of those leads working out. Although all six pillars work, it would be challenging for one pillar to supply all 100 leads required in that twelve-month period.

Let's go back to the Realtor who has all their eggs in one basket, which honestly is most Realtors. Let's say they migrated to working for sale-by-owners only; that's the thing they do that's what they are now known for in their Realtor community. Sally is the "for-sale-by-owner queen". The truth is that Sally is probably quite efficient with private sales, and that she has honed the skill of communicating the benefits of being on MLS, having the rest of the Real Estate community working on their behalf for a quicker sale, probably for more money. A lot safer and more secure, with all her Is dotted and Ts crossed, Sally has an excellent pillar. However, Sally still has a problem: her annual goal is twenty-five transactions. Sally needs to move twenty-five families to achieve her goal and, although her efforts in working private sales will be productive, it's a bit of a stretch for Sally to work closely with 100 for-sale-by-owner leads in the time allotted to achieve her goal. What Sally needs are another two pillars that are just as productive as her plan that she already follows with her private sales.

This brings us back to step two of the magic formula, *working three pillars*. What if Sally only needed twenty-five leads from for-sale-by-owners in a twelve-month period, twenty-five leads from a secondary pillar, and twenty-five leads from a third pillar? That would be seventy-five of the required 100. There are always some random leads annually—not a fourth pillar, just random leads from sign calls, ad calls, and referrals. Maybe Sally doesn't choose open houses but she holds properties open periodically.

This is a much more predictable, duplicable plan for Sally to achieve her twelve-month goal to assist twenty-five families to achieve their personal goal of buying or selling a home. If you think this through, it's really quite simple to sell twenty-five homes annually—you simply need twenty-five leads from each pillar and the other twenty-five random leads up to the required 100 will find you. That's really just two leads per month on average from each pillar. This doesn't necessarily include qualified listing appointments or Buyer's agreements signed—this only means a couple of people per month saying to you, "Yes, we are thinking about buying or selling in the next ninety days." So, let's say Sally chooses to work with her past clients and centre of influence as her number one pillar, which is mandatory in our coaching program. For her second and third pillars, Sally decides on the private sales (I also refer to this as "for-sale-by-owners"), which is already in her business model, along with geographical farming to complete the proper business model of working three pillars.

Example: Sally's proper business model that cannot fail:

Sources of Leads	Annual Leads Required
Pillar #1 Past clients and centre of influence	25
Pillar #2 For-sale-by-owners (private sales)	25
Pillar #3 Geographical farming	25
Randomly sourced leads	25
TOTAL LEADS	100

It's important to note that pillars two and three are interchangeable. Sally may have chosen open houses as Pillar #2 and previously listed properties ("expired listings") as her Pillar #3. All the pillars work—they all just need to provide a total leads number equal to Sally's desired annual goal. Therefore, if Sally has a goal of thirty sales annually, assisting thirty families to either buy or sell in a twelve-month period, nothing changes except for the math. In this case, thirty leads would be required from each of the pillars chosen, as well as thirty leads from random sources. The amount of leads required from random sources will always follow along with the annual goal. If the annual goal is twenty-five transactions, then the group of random leads will be twenty-five. If the annual goal is thirty transactions, then with the increased production the amount of random leads will follow along and be thirty.

So, if Sally set a real big goal of fifty transactions annually, that would probably rank her in the top 1 percent of any marketplace—maybe even the top ½ percent. Sally would definitely be a force to be reckoned with. Statistically, very few Realtors ever accomplish that kind of production. Sally could experience a profitable, rewarding career with a lot less than fifty transactions annually, but for fun, let's see what would be required for Sally to complete fifty transactions in a twelve-month period. Sally would need to work three pillars and get a lead each week from each pillar: fifty leads from Pillar #1, fifty leads from Pillar #2, and fifty leads from Pillar #3. At this production level, the group of random leads would be higher—in this scenario, fifty, which is equal to her annual goal.

It's funny when I'm teaching this in a seminar format and I'm explaining how this all works, I have a captive audience because as I'm explaining this system, "the magic formula", the Realtors look at me, listening and realizing that this is absolutely true and the mistakes they have been making are glaringly obvious, such as putting all their eggs in one basket, versus working three pillars. I always ask them this question: "If you worked a pillar five days a week, let's say you chose geographical farming and you committed one hour per day to either calling or door knocking in your farm, do you think you would get a lead once a week?" They think for a minute, then usually say that probably sounds reasonable. "Okay, so if you did that for each pillar and committed one hour of either calling or door knocking in that pillar, then each pillar would give you about fifty leads per year to go along with the fifty random leads that would accompany your volume of production."

At this point, someone in the class usually comments that I make this sound too easy, to find a lead in each pillar weekly and accomplish fifty transactions and be a Real Estate icon in the community. Of course I make it sound easy, because that is the way it works, and that's why it's called the magic formula. I've done it personally and we have hundreds of clients at this level or a greater production level. I mentioned earlier that an amazing career could be accomplished with a lot less than fifty transactions annually. Just do the appropriate math; eighty leads equals twenty transactions, 100 leads equals twenty-five transactions, 120 leads equals thirty transactions, and so on.

I had a great conversation about six months ago with a client from Ottawa. She called me because she thought that the process sounded too simple and that maybe she was missing something. She is a new Realtor and was looking to launch an awesome fulfilling career as a Real Estate professional. Her production goal for her first year was twenty transactions. Based on the average selling price in her market, twenty transactions would translate into about $140,000 gross income—a very good start to her career. If a Realtor successfully closes twenty transactions in their first year, that would not go unnoticed in this profession. Even though this wasn't her motivation, it is always nice to be recognized as a legitimate player in the bigger game. Several months went by and, although she went to the office everyday and did what she thought were the right things to do, she was beginning to think that maybe this dream either might not happen or at least would be more elusive than she had first imagined.

While out for lunch with a fellow Realtor, she mentioned that her start to this new career wasn't quite going as planned. Her lunch partner asked if she had considered Real Estate coaching, to which she admitted she didn't know there was such a thing. Lucky for her, the Realtor she was having lunch with happened to be a client of ours and has been working our system for a couple of years. This Realtor mentioned that she was also struggling a few years ago and that now she focuses on finding ten leads every month, which adds up to 120 annually and translates to thirty sales annually. Upon hearing this, the new Ottawa Realtor realized that was the kind of focus she needed—to find a certain number of leads monthly. Her lunch partner then suggested that the number of leads for her to focus on each month is six.

A few days later, she joined our coaching program and was assigned to one of our awesome coaches, who expanded on that lunchtime conversation. This brings me back to the conversation I had with her about six months ago. She called me to say my coach was making this sound a little too easy and she wanted to make sure she wasn't missing something. "According to my coach," she said, "if I want to sell twenty homes in the next twelve months, I require eighty leads because one in four work out. Basically, I need six leads per month more or less, and I find those leads from working my three pillars, the first of which is my past clients and centre of influence. My second pillar is open houses and my third is a geographical farm. So, according to my coach, these three sources will give me eighty leads and I'll achieve my goal of twenty sales—is that correct?"

"Well, that's not quite correct," I replied.

"I thought so, I knew I was missing something."

"Well, the part you are missing, or not quite connecting, makes it simpler—not more challenging. Every year some leads will find you, maybe one or two per month, equalling fifteen or so per year. You were thinking it sounded too easy that your three pillars supply eighty leads annually and you would turn those eighty leads into twenty transactions and launch your Real Estate career. In fact, your pillars only need to supply around sixty-five leads, which are added to the fifteen or so that find you. This will equal up to eighty."

"I called you thinking that I had missed a piece of the puzzle because it sounded a little too simple for me to get eighty leads from three pillars, but in fact I only need about sixty-five leads from my three pillars to put together with the fifteen that will find me?"

"Correct," was my response. "That's why it's called the magic formula!"

Now, six months after this conversation, I'm happy to say that this young lady, in working her three pillars and following her coach's instructions, has found forty-two leads and has eleven sales slightly ahead of schedule. It's amazing how simple this business is when we focus on working three Pillars and finding the appropriate number of leads monthly.

Let's take a look at how each of the six pillars work.

PILLAR #1: PAST CLIENTS AND CENTRE OF INFLUENCE

There are a couple of interesting things you need to know about this group of people before I explain how the plan works.

Interesting point #1: They think you are rich!

Me—rich! Nothing could be further from the truth. However, that doesn't change the fact that they certainly do think that you are rich. You might wonder, *How did they get that idea?* Well, all Realtors have something in common: they pretend they are doing a bit better than they are. Think about it—every time you run into someone from your database at the mall or at a function, the first thing they ask is, "How's the market?" To which you reply, "Oh, my gosh, the market is incredible. Things are selling very fast, some for over the asking price." You don't then add in, *For me, unfortunately, I haven't listed or sold anything for a couple of months*. Of course you don't say that—that would be crazy and unwise. Fake it till you make it. You might be a better salesperson than you are giving yourself credit for.

So, you run into them and they ask about the market? If you tell them how amazing things are, then they leave the conversation with the impression that you are doing really well—"Congrats on your amazing sales skills." Unfortunately perhaps you are not doing really well but they think you are. You are not doing something wrong here; in fact, you are doing the right thing. You are supposed to portray the essence of success, which would probably make things sound a little rosier than they truly are. The problem isn't that you pretend you are doing better than you are—the problem is that you are leaving them with what in most cases would be an illusion, and leaving them in that state of mind. You see, if your database thinks you are rich, but you never call them and talk about business, then you have accidently trained your database to not send you referrals because you're already so successful without them.

Think about it—you run into them, they ask about the market, you tell them how wonderful things are, and they leave the conversation thinking, *Wow, Bob is doing really well.* In fact, Bob hasn't listed or sold anything in sixty days and Bob is actually struggling. The problem with this all-too-common scenario is that Realtor Bob needs referrals from his past clients and centre of influence. Bob is acutely aware that referrals from this group of people are the backbone of every Realtor. Unfortunately, Bob has trained this group to not send him referrals. This brings me to the second thing you need to know about this group.

Interesting point #2: They are trained to not send you referrals

If you think this through, you will see that I am correct. Fortunately we teach a very simple solution to fix this problem. If your past clients and centre of influence, the most important group of people in your business, think you are rich, then they are unaware that you require their assistance to achieve the annual goal you have set. They won't send you referrals out of respect. Think about the magnitude of what I am explaining here.

This database is your past clients and centre of influence, your number one pillar, the backbone of every Realtor's business, and they are the group of people that, without whose cooperation and input into your business, will render the achieving of your goal almost impossible. They are the group that has the capacity to make the difference between an amazing or a continually challenging career. If they think you are rich and very, very, very busy, which is the impression we give them, they will not send you leads.

Statistically, every adult in North America knows two people moving every year. Perhaps a work colleague will mention over lunch that a move is in their plans. This is one of the two they know this year; obviously you would love them to say, "Hey do you have a Realtor? Because I know a great one." Well, unfortunately, you now have your database trained to not send you referrals by leading them to think that you're doing better than you are. So, out of respect for you, they will not mention you to this prospective client because in their mind you are too busy and this referral would probably be a burden to you.

Your database of course does send you some referrals; however, listen carefully to the words they choose when they do. When they send you a referral, the conversation usually goes like this.

"Hi, Bob, it's Mark. How are you?"

"Very good," responds Realtor Bob, "great to hear from you."

"I have a colleague who is thinking about selling their home and buying another. I know you are *really busy*, but do you think you can fit them in?"

"Fit them in?" Bob will say. "Of course, that's what I do for a living! Actually, I need these people right now—I'm in a bit of a slump, so maybe they can get me out."

If you have been selling for a while and you are honest with yourself, you will see that they make it sound as if you are doing them some kind of favour by selling their colleague's home and getting them another. Again, the words they chose included their illusion that you are *really busy*. It's fine that they think you are doing a little better than your actual situation; however, you must let them know that you are looking for referrals. Fortunately, I have the solution.

Interesting point #3: Real Estate is everyone's favourite topic

North America is seen as the land of opportunity and it truly is. It has been said that the streets are paved with gold. If you have the ambition to accomplish something, then this is definitely the place. But it probably won't come to you—you still need to go and get it, but it's there for the taking.

When we hear the term "living the dream", where does your mind go? What do we think about? For many people it's about being an entrepreneur, making lots of money, being your own boss, and operating above the everyday grind that most folks endure. Owning Real Estate is a big piece of that puzzle. It's a piece of the North American dream. Statistically, up to 95 percent of the millionaires in North America got there by way of Real Estate holdings. Owning and accumulating Real Estate is by far the most predictable path for wealth. Owning Real Estate is built into the conscious and subconscious fabric of North America. The desire to own Real Estate is part of our culture. It's almost everyone's goal.

It's very convenient that is what you do for a living. Selling Real Estate is a large portion of the bigger picture for the entire population of your country. Every adult has a strong desire to own Real Estate and then maybe some more. It's no wonder every time you see someone from your past clients or centre of influence at the mall that the first thing they say to you is, "Hey, how's the market?" If you really think about it, it's kind of rude of them. They should really say, "I'm sorry, let's back it up. How are you?" They don't, of course, and we are obviously okay with it. The truth is it's such a part of our psychological make up that they can't help themselves. What you do for a living is part of their inner drive to acquire Real Estate, maybe multiple units, and achieve financial wealth.

This would also explain why the Real Estate shows on TV are so popular, be it about listing it, loving it, renovating it—it doesn't matter. Any show about everyone's favourite topic is an automatic hit.

On a side note, it's interesting that over the years of training and coaching, literally thousands of Realtors have told me that they can't call their past clients and centre of influence on a regular basis because they feel like they're bugging them or begging for business. Really, what you do for a living is at the very core of everyone that lives in North America—when their phone rings, they hope it's their family or you, their Realtor. If you read this and you think, *You know, I think I fit into that category. I definitely feel like I'm bugging or annoying them*, take a few minutes, reread this point, and understand the magnitude of how dependent your clients are at their core on the topic of Real Estate, to which you are an expert.

Interesting point #4: They need an outlet

This point is really interesting and one that every Realtor needs to be acutely aware of. Your database needs an outlet. They have a strong desire to have Real Estate conversations because it's built into the very core of our being. Your spouse may be a lawyer or a doctor, but the odds are that doesn't come up in conversation when you see someone from your database at the mall. Why? These professions are not part of the inner culture, unlike Real Estate, which everyone wants to talk about.

This means that your clients will need to have some regular conversations with you in an organized fashion, which I will explain later. First, I need to help you get over your mental hang-ups. There's no point in giving you the plan if you are going to hold onto that feeling of, "I'd love to call them but I feel like I'm bothering them." I must first make you realize how crazy that is, be it very common. Do you think when someone sees you at an event of some sort that they think, *Oh, here comes Realtor Bob, he's probably going to bring up Real Estate so I might as well beat him to the punch*? Of course that's not happening. You know that their inquiry is genuine. They are clearly interested in what you know. You know this is true.

When I'm teaching this in a seminar format, I ask the audience, "So, if we know this is true, that they genuinely have a sincere interest in what we know, then where does the feeling that you're bugging them come from?" The room is usually filled with puzzled looks. I usually then say, "You're looking at me like cows watching a train go by—if you grew up on a farm, you know what I'm talking about. I'm saying that everyone in your database has an insatiable appetite to talk about Real Estate, and if you're not the conduit, someone else will be." I'm going to give you the plan but, first things first, if you hold onto the thought that you're bugging them, then you won't be able to implement the program that I'm going to share with you.

Interesting point #5: The payoff

The payoff is what you can expect to receive if you work this particular pillar correctly, which is 10 percent annually. So, if your past clients and centre of influence database has 100 people then the annual transactions will be ten from this pillar. If your database has 200 people then the annual transactions would be twenty from this pillar. Of course, I am just discussing this pillar—the other two pillars would also produce transactions and then of course a few random deals.

For example, the following chart is based on 100 people in your Pillar#1 database:

Pillars	Annual Transactions
Pillar #1 Past clients and centre of influence	10
Pillar #2 Geographical farming	8
Pillar #3 For-sale-by-owners (private sales)	7
Some random transactions	5
TOTAL TRANSACTIONS	**30**

As you can see, your past clients and centre of influence is just part of the overall goal. Again, this chart is based on 100 people in your database. Of course, if your database was 200 people, then twenty transactions would be beside Pillar #1, and Pillar #2 and Pillar #3 would remain the same.

When I teach this in a class setting, the students listen, but they're thinking, *This sounds too good to be true*. They often ask, "So are you saying that you're going to show us how to get twenty transactions from 200 people every year, year after year?" I respond with, "That is exactly what I'm going to teach you. I know that this does sound like a bit of a stretch compared to where you are right now, but let me share something with you that will open your mind and help you understand that what I'm teaching will definitely happen." I then have a captive audience as they realize the magnitude of what I'm sharing and the impact it could have on their business and, in turn, on their lives and the lives of their families.

I say to the group, "I would like you to write something down. According to board statistics, every adult in North America knows two people buying or selling every year." That statistic is very easy for a Realtor to accept. In fact, that fact might be a little conservative. So I pick someone out of the group and I ask them, "How big is your database?"

They respond, "Two hundred."

"Are you currently getting twenty transactions annually from those 200? Not twenty transactions total in your business, but specifically from those 200?"

"No." This is always the answer.

"Approximately how many transactions are you receiving from those 200?"

"Four to seven." These are the usual numbers.

"So, for me to tell you that I can show you how to increase that number from four to seven to twenty, that would be exciting." Again, the look of *this sounds too good to be true* resurfaces on their countenance. "Can you accept the statistic that every adult knows two people buying or selling every year?

Again, "Yes."

"Okay, so that means that your 200 people will know 400 people moving this year, and 400 moving next year, and the year after that, and on and on for the rest of your career. Don't you think that if you talked to your people on a regular basis—those same people that have an insatiable appetite to discuss Real Estate—that you could capture twenty out of 400? If you follow what I'm teaching I can show you how to lose 380 transactions out of 400. That sounds a little negative, but it's still the same math."

At this point I have the whole group on side. You should be on side as well if you have 200 names in your database and you know that they will know 400 people moving every year, so it's very reasonable to capture twenty. Usually at this point someone in the class puts their hand up and asks a really good question: "My people already know I'm a good Realtor—why am I not getting that amount of referrals?"

"Good question. The answer is they think you are rich and they are currently being respectful of your time, so you have accidentally trained your people to not send you referrals. As soon as you work the plan, the switch will be made and you will receive the allotted number of transactions annually." This brings me to *the plan*.

The plan

The plan for this pillar is quite simple with amazing results, which are about 10 percent annually. Just as a reminder, when you have 200 names in your past clients and centre of influence database, then the payoff is twenty transactions annually, which is 10 percent. When those transactions are coupled with the transactions earned from your second and third pillars, I think that you will finally have the Real Estate business that you have been searching for.

My plan for this process may seem too simple for you, but I can assure you that it has worked for all our clients, so be assured it will work for you as well. I am aware that there are many Real

Estate coaching and training programs available to you and most teach a much more complex plan for working and servicing this most important group of people, "valued clients". However, in many cases, simpler is better, and that concept applies here. I'm saying that if you will adhere to these six simple steps, you will achieve your goal of 10 percent in this pillar.

Step #1: Get everyone in your database that belongs there
Step #2: Divide into eleven equal pieces
Step #3: Call one piece each week
Step #4: Leave a message at the end of the week for those not reached
Step #5: Mail or email monthly
Step #6: Add ten names monthly

You might be thinking that these six steps seem like a pretty simple process to achieving your desired goal in the pillar of past clients and centre of influence. Well, you would be correct. If you implement these six simple steps, your goal of 10 percent annually would be achieved. Keep in mind you have two other pillars to work and each of those pillars also has a simple plan of five or six points. I would recommend you just do these six points and Pillar #1 will be perfect.

Anything you do above and beyond these six points won't make much of a difference as far as production is concerned. This means that a lot of Realtors buy their clients gifts after the sale, which is fine. We certainly don't suggest our clients stop this practice, but you're not getting anything for it. I'm sure they appreciate the gesture and maybe you enjoy the process. Be clear, Realtor, if you have 200 names in a database and you work the six simple steps you will in turn receive 10 percent return—twenty transactions.

If you also buy them a gift, your return will pretty much be the same. This is factual. We tested it over and over. So, my advice would be if you enjoy the process of giving gifts, then by all means, continue. However, if you're in the habit of buying gifts and don't want to, then just stop. I'm only using buying gifts as an example. Anything above and beyond the six-step plan would be in the same boat, for example, helping them move, or taking them for lunch or dinner. Maybe you like these activities, and that's fine—continue doing them. I'm just pointing out that you are not going to move the margin of transactions by doing anything like this, and you do have two other pillars that also need your attention.

Let's take a look at each of the six steps in the plan to be sure you are clear on how they work.

Step #1: Get everyone in your database that belongs there

The guideline for who should be in your database is, if they are an adult and they would know who you are when you call, then they should be on your list. Most Realtors make a mistake of only having their favourite fifty and that's the folks they work. That's a huge mistake. Let's say you consider a name: "John". John doesn't have a great job and probably isn't in the market for a house, maybe ever, so you decide not to add him to your database even though he fits the guideline—he's an adult and he would know who you are when you call. You should add him anyway. You are probably correct that John won't be in the market anytime soon, but his older brother or sister, who are in a much better financial situation, might have a move on the horizon, or maybe his parents, or a buddy from work. John might be an amazing referral source but, because most Realtors keep their database small, John won't make their cut. If a person knows who you are, they should be on the list. A 250-person database is much better than a 100-person database. That's twenty-five transactions versus ten transactions. The additional 150 people will hold several people like John.

Step #2: Divide into eleven equal pieces

Realtors always ask me, "Why divide my database into eleven pieces? There are thirteen weeks in a ninety-day cycle." That's true, but there is a really good reason behind eleven pieces. We teach eight weeks vacation annually. That equates to forty-four weeks of work. We want you to call your database every ninety days. With two weeks vacation every ninety days, this breaks your database into eleven equal pieces, which will allow you to stay on track and not fall behind.

Step #3: Call one piece each week

It's possible that this might be the most important piece of the entire puzzle. If a Realtor printed off their database with the intention to call them in the next ninety days, they would probably start with their favourites. Of course, this would be easy for the first few weeks or month, but then would be difficult to finish. The solution is simple: break your database into eleven equal pieces and call one piece each week. If your database consists of 200 names and you divide that by eleven, you will have eleven groups of about eighteen names. In week one, call the first group, then in week two, call the second group, and so on. This is the only way to avoid calling your favourites all at once.

Step #4: Leave a message at the end of the week for those not reached

The objective here is to reach your people. It's much better if you talk to them, but when they get your message they'll be aware that you are looking for business, thus solving the problem of them thinking that you are already rich and not in need of any assistance.

The goal would be to have a conversation with about 70 percent of the clients that are allocated to this week and leave about 30 percent of them a message.

It would work like this: your database is 200 people and 1/11th is eighteen people—that's who you reach out to this week. You try them all week without leaving a message, and on Friday you leave them a message and move on to the next group of eighteen next week. So, on Friday, you hit the goal of having a conversation with twelve or thirteen people and you leave five or six voicemails. Mission accomplished.

When I teach this in a seminar format, without question someone will ask, "If they see you're calling and not leaving a message, and they then call you, how would you handle that?"

I respond, "That will definitely happen. In fact, it's very common. You simply say, 'Thanks for returning my call. Every time I called you I was heading into a meeting and did not want to start a game of telephone tag.' To which they will respond, 'Thank you very much, I appreciate that. I wish more people would think that way.' Then you just have the conversation with them that you would have had if they had answered the phone, and cross them off the list."

Later I will tell you what to say in this conversation. For now, keep reading. If you leave messages starting on Monday, you'd be leaving almost all messages again. It's much better if you do your very best to reach them. So, try them all week and leave a message on Friday. It's important that you follow this process so that things don't break down. You must leave messages on Friday. Be sure not to carry anyone over to the next week—this would pose a problem in the near future and cause the whole process to come to a screeching stop. If you don't leave messages on Friday for those not reached and just move to the new group on Monday, what will happen is that you'll have a new group of 1/11th on Monday plus six from last week, four from the previous week, two from the week before that, and there's your screeching stop. To keep the process flowing easily, make sure every Friday you leave a message for those not reached and make it your goal to talk to about 70 percent of them. No one is perfect, so make the goal to not to exceed a 20-percent margin for error.

A 20-percent margin for error means approximately eight of the eleven weeks go off without a hitch. You speak to twelve or thirteen and leave five or six messages. This also means that approximately three times you get to Friday and, due to valid reasons, you have only talked to two. Perhaps either you were sick, your kids were sick, company from out of town was visiting; it doesn't matter what the reason was, but it's Friday, and calling this 1/11th didn't go well. Leave all the messages on Friday and move along to the next group the following Monday. It's better to cut your losses and stay in the system. There's an important note here: if on Friday you had a bad week and you're left with more than the 20-percent margin for error, then you are not trying hard enough. Elevate your game.

Step #5: Mail or email monthly

You have a choice here to either mail or email a flyer to your database monthly. Both will work effectively. Of course, the big difference is that mailing to your database does carry a significant cost, and emailing is low cost or free. You could create your own hard cover flyer for mailing versus hiring a company to do this service for you. However, if you calculate the hours to create the flyer, you are probably better to have a company do it for you. Plus, their finished product will probably be superior to your efforts.

The thing that you want to consider is this: as you read this plan, if you are honest with yourself, you have probably been somewhat negligent in your efforts to stay in touch with this most important group of folks, your past clients and centre of influence. This means that either your whole plan or most of your plan has been mailing to your database monthly through a service and that's it. If you do call your database, you probably have only been calling your favourites. The mailing of the professional flyer made sense, but once you implement the calling in groups, then that calling will become the program and the monthly flyer will just be a supplement piece. In this case, hard copy and email flyer have the same result. Most of our clients have converted to the email flyer monthly as opposed to the hard copy flyer and they get the same result, which is a 10 percent return.

If you read this and for some reason decide not to call your database in groups of $1/11^{th}$ then your flyer would be your entire program. In this case I would suggest the hard copy flyer over the email flyer. So, in essence, you would take on the expense in order to not do your job correctly and, in turn, probably get six or seven transactions from your 200-person database versus twenty transactions annually. That's a big price to pay for whatever hang up you are carrying in your head. On top of that, you are letting transactions happen with other Realtors who might not treat them as well as you would. You shouldn't let that happen. I highly recommend you call your database every ninety days in $1/11^{th}$ groups so they can be safe with you.

Step #6: Add ten names monthly

I meet Realtors all the time. At the time of writing of this book, I host approximately 350 seminars annually so I interact with thousands upon thousands of Realtors every calendar year. Our model is three pillars with the past clients and centre of influence as the number one pillar, so I always ask Realtors how large their database is and how long they have been selling. It's interesting how many inform me that they have been selling for ten years and they have 100 in their past clients and centre of influence database. For whatever reason, they don't connect the importance of having a larger database.

100 person database = 10 annual transactions
200 person database = 20 annual transactions
300 person database = 30 annual transactions
400 person database = 40 annual transactions

We tend to think the bigger the database the more difficult it seems to achieve the 10 percent annually. Somehow we think that achieving ten transactions from 100 people is easier than achieving 100 transactions from 1,000 people. Of course the math is exactly the same—it's your brain playing tricks on you. The only difference would be the size of the elevenths allocated weekly.

Most of our clients make about twenty contacts daily. If the database is smaller, they make more contacts in pillars two and three. When the database grows, they make fewer contacts in pillars two and three and the same twenty contacts daily. To the Realtors with small databases, look at it this way: you can't put toothpaste back in a tube – start growing it. I would like you to follow this guideline. You don't have to go from zero to hero, you don't need to go on a campaign to grow your database in the next sixty days, but just start adhering to this point: *add ten names per month.* If your database right now is 100 and you add ten monthly, that's 120 yearly. In one year your database will grow to 220, then in another year 340, then 460, and so on. As mentioned, nothing will change in your prospecting, just less calls in pillars two and three and more calls in the all-important pillar of your past clients and centre of influence.

So, how do you add those ten names monthly and who are these people? The improper way to grow your database would be to put the people that you talk to while prospecting that you had good conversations with, or the nice people who came into your open house. If you do add these folks in, you will be constantly purging your database. This will lead to endless frustration and will keep you out of your database altogether.

Every Real Estate coaching and training company calls this group your past clients and centre of influence. When a nice person comes into your open house, that doesn't make them a past client or a centre of influence. That makes them a nice person who came into your open house. That's it. They might be a lead, that's true—I haven't gotten to how to process them yet, but it's coming up. They may in fact buy or sell through you, in which case they are now a past client and entered into your database; however, when they enter your open house, they are neither a past client nor a centre of influence at this point.

Here's what will happen if you enter these folks into your database. For example, a nice lady comes into your open house. You have a nice chat with her, she gives you her data, and you enter her into your database. A month or two later, her name comes up in the appropriate eleventh. You call her, her husband answers the phone, and you try to strike up a conversation. He stops you and asks, "Who are you?" You try to explain but he cuts you off with the statement, "We are not interested in selling." This of course makes it a bit difficult to make the next call. The truth is they shouldn't have been there in the first place, but that's an error on your part.

Don't feel bad. Most Realtors have made this mistake, including me in my early years. I have a solution for this very common problem. In fact, it's so common almost every Realtor we have the privilege to coach has made this mistake, which means when we get them they have a whole bunch of names in their database that shouldn't be there. We know as a coaching company that when we get them on our system, selecting three pillars with their database as number one, they learn exactly how we want them to work each of the pillars. If they have a big group of names in their database that they really don't know, that will keep them out of their database altogether. So, for us, that's a problem. They know the system but are unable to work it, which means they would be in coaching and not achieving—that doesn't work for us. The solution is quite simple if they're aware of what they're doing and why. That helps them to correct the problem.

Simply break your database into eleven equal pieces. In week one, call everyone and eliminate those who shouldn't be there in the first place. In week two, do the same process. Once you have completed a ninety-day cycle, your database will be correctly purged. Then, don't make that common mistake again.

This brings me to how we add ten names per month. Who are these people and where do they come from? There are several correct ways to add names to your database. Obviously, when you sell someone something, you will add them. However, you can also make sales and not add these clients to your database. If a past client lists their home with you that you sold them five years ago, you have a new sale, but you haven't added anyone to your database. They were already there. In fact, they might sell and buy twice, but you still didn't add anyone to your database because they were already there. FYI, if you call your database every ninety days in groups of elevenths, that scenario will happen a lot more frequently.

To add names to your database through past clients, you would need to make sales with people that are not currently in your database. Ten of them monthly would be challenge, which means that the bulk of the people added to your database will be almost entirely from the centre of influence category. I have a couple of ideas here that worked well for me and are working quite nicely for thousands of Realtors around North America, assisting them in adding ten names per month.

Idea #1: At all functions get used to saying this script

"The market is always busy. I do stay in touch with the folks I know several times per year so they know what's going on in the crazy market. I would be happy to stay in touch with you."

You know that because you are a Realtor, every time you are anywhere at any function—be it a wedding, a fiftieth birthday party, really any function—every time someone sees you, it's, "Hey, Bob, how's the market?" You simply respond with the above script. Note there is no mention of your mailing list or your database or even the fact that you will be calling four times per year. We have to make sure we are choosing words that are easy to say yes to. At a function when someone says, "Hey, how's the market?", if you say, "I could add you to my calling list" or "I could add you to my database" or "I could call you four times a year", the response to those words would be, "No, that's okay." You chose words that are difficult to say yes to. It's better to choose words that are easy to say yes to like,

"The market is always busy. I do stay in touch with the folks I know several times per year so they know what's going on in the crazy market. I would be happy to stay in touch with you."

To which they would respond, "Would you? That would be awesome." And you'd say, "I would be happy to. Do you have a card?" If they have a card they will say, "Absolutely," and they will give you their card. If they don't have a card, then just pull one out of your pocket and say, "Write your name, cell, and email on the back." If your Real Estate cards are not blank on the back, order a small amount, maybe 100 or so, solely for this purpose.

I remember as a young Realtor I was interested in growing my database correctly with people that actually did want to talk to me periodically. Every function I attended I always added four to six people to my database. The great thing is I didn't have to do anything except be there. It wasn't anything proactive on my part. Every time someone said, "Hey, Rob, how's the market?" I just responded,

"The market is always busy. I do stay in touch with the folks I know several times per year so they know what's going on in the crazy market. I would be happy to stay in touch with you."

To which they responded, "That would be awesome," and I carried on enjoying myself at whatever function I was at. When I got home I would empty my pockets and look at that six new people to add to my database who were okay with my periodic calling every ninety days.

Idea #2: Use the same scripts with people that you interact with during your regular day

As you travel through your normal day-to-day activities, use the exact same script:

"The market is always busy. I do stay in touch with the folks I know several times per year so they know what's going on in the crazy market. I would be happy to stay in touch with you."

If you think about it, the opportunities to grow your past clients and centre of influence are common and you will notice them if you are looking for them. Let's say you are working with a Buyer and she is looking to buy a condo. On one of your outings she brings a friend along, which is quite common. Up until now, you are pleasant with her friend as you spend the next couple of hours viewing condos. You may even give her friend your card for future use. However, now that you are focusing on the growth of your number one pillar, your past clients and centre of influence database, you have a much more direct conversation with your Buyer's friend. I'm not saying that you become overly aggressive and jump on the friend the moment they get into your car—after all, you have them for the next couple of hours.

Just wait for the friend to ask about the market. It will happen for sure. Then, respond with,

"The market is always busy. I do stay in touch with the folks I know several times per year so they know what's going on in the crazy market. I would be happy to stay in touch with you."

It's very simple, really. Obviously your Buyer's friend doesn't have a Realtor or your Buyer would probably be with that Realtor. Your Buyer's friend will most likely respond with, "That would be awesome."

Perhaps when you get an offer on one of your listings you call your Seller to say you will bring the offer over at 7:00 p.m. As you arrive, they have company, who immediately leave so you can conduct your business. You smile at them as they pass you in the hall and you get started with the negotiations of the offer. You make the sale and move along. However, now you have the constant growth of your database in your mind so you inquire who that family was that they were entertaining. "Oh that's my brother. He lives across town."

You respond, "My plan is to call you periodically so you know what's going on in the crazy market. I could offer your brother and his family the same service." Odds are, the brother doesn't have a Realtor or your client would have been listed for sale with the brother's Realtor.

Your client responds, "I think my brother would like that. Here is his number—give him a call."

You call the brother and say a very similar script:

"Hi ___, it's Bob from Go Get 'Em Realty. I wanted to let you know that we did in fact sell your brother's home conditionally last night."

"Yes I was aware. Congratulations!"

"The market is always busy. I do stay in touch with the folks I know several times per year so they know what's going on in the crazy market. I would be happy to stay in touch with you."

They will probably respond, "That would be great." Opportunities to grow your past clients and centre of influence database are all around you in your day-to-day business activities. Right now you are probably just not noticing them. If you have it in your head to add ten names to your database monthly, then you will take advantage of all the possibilities that currently surround you.

As you communicate with your past clients and centre of influence every ninety days in groups of $1/11^{th}$, it's important you say the right things in the right ways. You need to bring some value to the call, be it some information about the market or something connected to their immediate neighbourhood. It's also important that you follow a proper sequence in your dialogue. If you start the conversation personal and then shift the conversation to business, that's going to be very awkward. If you start the conversation out with, "How's the family? How's work?" or "How are the kids?" then they'll respond, "Fine, okay," all the time thinking, *What do you want?* Then when you upgrade the conversation to business they think, *Oh, that's why you called.* That's awkward for you and for them.

Personal to business = awkward

Fortunately, every coin has two sides, which means that if personal to business is awkward, then business to personal is comfortable. Conveniently for the Realtor, that's exactly the way it is.

Business to personal = comfortable

I'm not saying to be all business with your database—not at all. In my career, I have been very social with my clients. Just on the calls, I talk business first then personal. Not less personal, just business first. They prefer it that way and so will you. If you continue to open your calls on the personal level, it will become so uncomfortable for you that you will either abandon this pillar altogether and resort to sending them a calendar annually or, at best, only call the short list of your favourites. So, take the easy route for them and for you: business first then personal.

Example: Business portion first

> "Hi, is this ___?"
> "Yes."
> "Hi, ___, it's ___. Did I catch you at a good time?"
> "Yes."
> "I have a quick business call. Do you have a minute?"
> "Sure."

Example of business portion of the call

"I wanted to let you know that the market is quite busy right now. A lot of people are either buying or selling. I'm looking to assist some of those folks. So, who do you know that could use my assistance at this time?" Then, if they give you a name, say, "Would you mind if I gave them a call and could I mention your name?"

Example of personal portion of the call

"Thanks for always thinking about me I appreciate it."

"So how's work? How are the kids?"

And so on. This is your database, so you would know what you have in common. Given I live in Toronto, I'm a big Toronto Maple Leafs fan, so if I know my client is a Leaf fan I will bring up the Leafs. Or maybe we have golf or fishing in common, or our kids are in soccer—whatever it is, have some personal conversation and thank them for their time.

Personal to business = awkward

Business to personal = comfortable

It's also a very good idea to have some sort of annual event for this group of people. After all, it is your number one pillar and by far the most profitable of your three pillars. This is the collection of people that will either make or break you as a Realtor. It's a wise idea to invest some resources back into this group. Some ideas would be:

a) An investment seminar
b) Meet and greet at your club or office
c) Picnic
d) Rent a movie theatre

There are lots of ideas out there. My favourites are those connected to business. If you have never hosted an investment seminar, that's a really good idea. All you need to do is partner with someone, perhaps your mortgage broker or accountant, who is knowledgeable in this area to speak at your event, because there will be some possible business for them. They would usually be willing to share the cost or at least speak for free. I really like this idea because, whether the folks in your database have any interest or not, you still look good. When you invite them, it's a win-win for you.

You should always be looking to bring some value to the quarterly calls, so what could be better than saying to them, "I'm going to be hosting a free seminar on this date at this time for just my clients. We will have a guest speaker that will explain exactly how you can implement all the programs that are in place to help you become a Real Estate investor." If they have no interest, they say, "Thanks for the invite but no thanks," and you still look good in their eyes that you are supplying services like this to your clients. Or, perhaps they will have interest. Let's say you have 200 people in your past clients and centre of influence database and twenty are interested in attending your seminar. Congratulations, you now have an investment group of twenty. Hey, you have to call them every ninety days, so you might as well bring lots of value. They will appreciate it.

As a closing thought on this pillar: this is by far the most important of the six pillars. If you get this one right, it will be difficult to fail. On the other hand, if you ignore this pillar, it will be difficult to succeed.

PILLAR #2: GEOGRAPHICAL FARMING

First things first, let's take a look at why we call it "geographical farming". As Realtors we are familiar with the term *geographical farming*, but we might not give much thought to the origin of the phrase. In real farming, the farmer looks after the crops and animals. He cares for and nurtures them. That's the job of the farmer. Down the road he harvests his crops and stock for profit. If you think about it, that is exactly what geographical farming is for the

Realtor. You care for and nurture your farm, and make a profit. In this day and age, so many Realtors have forgotten the process. They have forgotten why it's called geographical farming. Most Realtors select a geographical area, drop flyers, and wait for the phone to ring. That's not geographical farming—that's geographical flyer delivery.

This process is lacking the caring for and nurturing of the neighbourhood. Could you imagine a farmer staying in his farmhouse and never going to the barn or field? Of course not—that would be crazy to think that an actual farmer would do that. Well, to select an area to specialize in and not take the time to get in there, knock on their doors, and get to know the people would be equally crazy. Yet, this is exactly what most Realtors do if they have farming as one of their lead sources. If you are unwilling to take the time on a regular organized basis to go to your farm and get to know the people, then I would highly recommend you do not select this pillar. On the other hand, if you are willing to do the necessary work, this pillar has the potential to be amazing. As a Realtor myself, I chose geographical farming as my second pillar and enjoyed the process of door knocking on a regular basis and, in turn, sold several hundred homes in my farm over my career.

The plan

Step #1: Select the correct neighbourhood
Step #2: Select the appropriate size
Step #3: Flyer delivery
Step #4: Organized door knocking or calling
Step #5: Community event

Let's take some time and see exactly how each of these steps works.

Step #1: Select the correct neighbourhood

It's funny, when I teach this in a seminar format, I ask the group, "Who has a geographical farm as a source of business?" There is always a group of hands that go up. It's a common activity. Interestingly, most confess at the end of the class that they have in fact a geographical flyer delivery area not a geographical farm. I then ask, "How many of you folks live in your farm area?" It's almost everyone. I then suggest that living there is not a criterion for selecting a geographical farm. I'm not suggesting that you cannot live in your farm—it's not the right selection process. It's possible that the location where the Realtor lives does meet the criteria, but if that is the case, then that's clearly a lucky break.

So, how do we select a farm? There is really just one item on the criteria list and that is annual turnover rate. If there are 1,000 homes in the farm and sixty sales annually, that's 6-percent turnover. A 6-percent annual turnover or better is our criterion for selection of a farm. Most Realtors start farming without even considering what the turnover rate is. I know this to be true because, during seminars when I ask who has a farm as a source of business and a bunch of hands go up, I discover afterwards that most live in their farm. I ask, "Who can tell me the turnover rate in their farm?" To date, no one has known the answer to the question. They usually ask, "What is a turnover rate?"

The turnover rate is quite easy to figure out. Simply put all the streets in your farm into the MLS system and set the computer back 365 days—one year—and hit the submit button. If you have 1,000 homes and you discover your farm has twenty-two sales annually, then it has a 2.2 percent turnover. Unfortunately, that's not a big enough pool of sales to make a pillar.

Again, most Realtors select where they live because they like the area. So, when they do this exercise and discover their neighbourhood has a 6 percent or better turnover rate, then that was simply luck. Be sure to take it when you get it. Unfortunately, most Realtors discover that the area they were farming simply does not have the annual turnover rate to support the activity. Usually they ask me, "What should I do? I've been farming here for four years." I respond, "Stop and select another area that has the correct turnover." It's unfortunate for sure. That's been a big waste of time and resources, but it's not going to change, so cut your losses and fix your mistake.

I can think very specifically about a client who we discovered very early in our coaching. She had made this very common mistake and was farming her neighbourhood that we discovered only had a 1.5 percent annual turnover rate: 800 residences and twelve sales annually. I explained to her that she couldn't make a pillar out of twelve possible sales. "I had one last year," she said. I responded, "You might get one next year again, but a sale every once in a while is not a pillar." I happened to know her area so I suggested she check the turnover rate of a series of townhouses not far from her home. "I don't like that area," was her response. "What's that got to do with it?" was my response.

Annual turnover is the criterion—not your likability factor of the area. Reluctantly she checked the area and got back to me with the news: 700 townhouses with fifty-six annual sales—an 8 percent annual turnover rate.

I asked her, "If you did the necessary work and got to know these people, how many of those fifty-six could you capture annually?"

"Maybe ten to fifteen," she replied.

I suggested that that would be an awesome pillar; she agreed. Fortunately, this young lady discontinued working the neighbourhood she lived in and focused her efforts on the more transient townhouse area. This story is four years old at the time of writing of this book, and I'm happy to report her geographical farm is in fact producing ten to fifteen sales annually.

You see, we need to spend a lot more attention on the turnover rate versus how much we like the area. We need to play the odds a little more. FYI, I don't like the area of my farm that I mentioned earlier, which of course has nothing to do with the process. Turnover is the key.

Step #2: Select the appropriate size

The proper size is about 1,000 homes. Keep in mind you have to get to know these people. If there are too many that would be challenging. It's very common for Realtors to tell me that their farm is 5,000 or 10,000 residences or even bigger. This is not geographical farming—it's geographical flyer delivery. Unfortunately, the cost of running a program that large is probably putting a strain on that Realtor's finances. Why not select a neighbourhood that meets the turnover rate of 6 percent or more and keep it at approximately 1,000 homes? That's a pool of sixty or more sales annually. And, while you're at it, enjoy the process of getting to know those folks and their families. Capture ten to fifteen sales annually and be a happy camper or, in this case, a happy farmer.

Step #3: Flyer Delivery

I recommend that, in order to make an impact as quickly as possible, you drop a flyer every two weeks for about six months, then monthly flyers from that point onwards. If you are fortunate enough to get a small foothold in the neighbourhood, and if you could manage to get a couple of listings in the first six months, then you can convert your flyer delivery from twice per month to monthly. It's really not that important what's on the flyer as long as it's professional. Let's face it, those who receive them don't keep them.

Periodically, Realtors tell me that they went to list a home in their geographical farm and the homeowner had their flyer in hand. Okay, that could happen every now and again, but overall and more commonly they see the flyer, glance at it, and throw it into the recycling bin. As long as they took mental note of your name and company, mission accomplished. With this in mind, it wouldn't make much sense to spend a lot of money or time on something that is going to be glanced at and tossed away. Again, as long as it looks professional, you're good. If you work at a Real Estate Franchise, odds are they already have some nice postcards or door hangers already prepared that would work just fine.

Step #4: Organized door knocking or calling

In the previous point, we talked about flyer delivery. This point is organized door knocking or telephone calling. This point, the door knocking or calling, is by far the more important of the two points. In fact, the flyer is merely a support piece. It's interesting that most Realtors around North America that work a geographical farm area drop flyers but never really call or door knock that particular neighbourhood. Once again, that's only geographical flyer delivery—not geographical farming. That will either not work at all or at least not work at the level it should. We need to make a commitment to break the farm up into manageable pieces and call or door knock one piece each week. If you are not willing to make this commitment, then I would highly recommend you choose a different pillar that you are willing to commit to.

Break the farm into fourteen manageable pieces that will have you calling or door knocking every home in your farm three times per year. One-third of a year is seventeen weeks. The reason I want you to break your farm into fourteen pieces is because we teach eight weeks vacation annually. So, every 120 days, there are three weeks vacation, hence seventeen weeks. In 120 days, your farm is broken into fourteen manageable pieces for you to either call or door knock. This way you won't fall behind when you allow for the allotted vacation time. It's common for Realtors to ask me which is better—to call or door knock the farm? Calling the farm will work for sure; however, it is much more effective to get out of your office and go over and meet the folks. For some pillars the phone is better, and for some the door. This one leans towards the door.

Step #5: Community event

If your farm is an actual community with a park, then an annual event in the park would be amazing. We have lots of clients who have hosted a movie night in the park or a daytime BBQ with face painting games and things to that effect. We also have clients who annually rent a movie theatre and host an event for their past clients and centre of influence. The seating capacity for most theatres is larger than the typical Realtor's database, so why not invite the farm and kill two birds with one stone? This is not a mandatory point to manage a geographical farm, but it is an awesome add on.

While communicating with the residents in your farm area, it's important not to make your calls or door knocking sound like a "just listed" or "just sold" call. The idea is to hold yourself out as the neighbourhood specialist. Once you are established and listing homes for sale is a regular occurrence for you, they will figure out on their own you are the local professional. However, it's a good idea to help them with this by talking to them right from the beginning in words that hold you out as the neighbourhood specialist.

> "Hi, is this ___?"
> "Yes."
> "Hi, ___, it's ___ from ___. How are you doing today?"

Take a sincere interest in their answer, and make the following points:

"Since we last talked, there have been twelve sales in the neighbourhood and they are averaging 98 percent of the asking price. Several have been on your street."

"I also wanted to remind you about the movie in the park coming up in September."

"While I have you at the door/on the phone, do you have any Real Estate questions?"

"Can I ask if a move would be in the near future for you?"

"Thanks for your time. I will catch up with you another time."

Geographical farming is a wonderful pillar. In real farming, the farmer plants in the spring and harvests in the fall. In geographical farming, once you plant and nurture the farm, you harvest all year round, and focus on the turnover rate!

PILLAR #3: FOR-SALE-BY-OWNERS

For-sale-by-owners are an interesting group for sure. Most Realtors don't possess the confidence to work this particular group. If you pay attention to what we teach here, this group will become a lot easier, for sure. When I was an active Realtor, I had this group as my third pillar and I quite enjoyed them. Of course, I had to figure out the right plan, which I will share with you and, in turn, help you to master these folks.

Most Realtors think that for-sale-by-owners are mean people who hate Realtors and would never pay commission. Although it is true that private sales are trying to save the commission, it would be a mistake to think that they won't pay commission at some point in the future. It's been my findings that about 20 percent of private sales do in fact hate Realtors and would die before they would pay any sort of a decent commission. However, that leaves 80 percent who are not like that at all. I've experienced that the 80 percent of the private sales I worked with were no more difficult to get commission from than any other person.

I'm not saying that just because the 80 percent are good to work with that you will get them listed. If you work the plan I will teach you shortly you will of course convert one in four. As far as the 20 percent that don't particularly appreciate what you do for a living, my plan doesn't involve working those folks. Sometimes Realtors ask me, "How will I know if they are in the 20 percent or the 80 percent?" Trust me, you will know. The 20 percent won't hide the fact that in their mind your job is totally irrelevant. Just wish them a nice day and move along and focus on the 80 percent. Actually, the 80 percent probably have already decided the date they will list on MLS. If you ask them, they will probably tell you.

The plan

Step #1: Talk to three new private sales every work day
Step #2: Separate those to work with ("court")
Step #3: Drop off the "How to save the commission" report
Step #4: Court correctly

Now, let's take a close look at how each of these points work.

Step #1: Talk to three new private sales every working day

You will notice that my program overall is not a workaholic program. That is clearly not my philosophy. If you choose for-sale-by-owners as a pillar, I just need you to talk to three new private sales daily. When I say 'new' I mean new to you—not private sales that you had spoken to on a previous day and now have in lead follow up.

Our program teaches eight weeks vacation, so I want you to work 220 days annually and speak to three for-sale-by-owners every working day. Over the year that would have you communicating with around 600 for-sale-by-owners annually. About 20 percent of them will be, as previously mentioned, hardened for-sale-by-owners and they will make that very clear on the phone or at their door in the first thirty seconds. I would highly recommend that you thank them for their time, wish them luck, and move along and never think about them again as long as you live.

However, that leaves the 80 percent—somewhere between 400 and 500 private sales to work with. I know that number seems high, but believe me, if you live in a city there probably are that many. If you live in a rural area or town obviously there probably wouldn't be enough private sales to consider it a pillar. Just call the few you have and implement this simple program. Of the remaining 400 to 500, the 80 percent, the objective would be to keep your eye on what you are trying to accomplish.

This is a secondary pillar to your past clients and centre of influence. So, ten to fifteen transactions annually from this pillar would be amazing. I know there are some programs that teach you to put all your leads on some sort of contact program, but I would highly recommend you don't do that. Trying to work the 80 percent, 400 to 500, is too big of a task and would only serve as a massive headache for you. On top of that, you would not be working your other two pillars because of all the work connected with trying to work 400 to 500 private sales. Instead, it's best to separate forty to sixty over the year and work them correctly, having that funnel down to ten to fifteen transactions. Remember, one in four leads works out. Again, ten to fifteen transactions from this pillar leaves you lots of time to work your other two pillars, and each of those pillars is also kicking in ten to fifteen transactions.

Step #2: Separate those to work with ("court")

When I use the term "court" in this context, I'm talking about the reference to old style dating known as "courting". In old style dating, "courting", the one doing the courting would move slowly and do their best to make a good impression. When working with for-sale-by-owners, it's much better to court, "work with", forty to sixty correctly and funnel that forty to sixty down to ten to fifteen transactions, which is an excellent pillar coupled with the other two pillars having a similar result.

Every Realtor who tries to work too many for-sale-by-owners at one time is on a collision course with frustration and, as an added negative result, will stop working their other two pillars. We get this a lot in our coaching program. When a client repeatedly asks their coach questions connected to the for-sale-by-owners pillar, the coach, suspecting that the client is trying to work too many private sales and neglecting their other two pillars, will inquire about the other two pillars. The common response is, "I'm a little bogged down with private sales, so I'm a bit behind with my other two pillars." The coach then suggests they should be a little more selective with which private sales they work and stay on track with each pillar.

If this particular client's annual goal is thirty transactions per year, the coach would remind them that if each pillar generated eight transactions, then that would be twenty-four, and the remaining six would come from random areas such as sign calls, internet calls, ad calls, and so on. The coach would remind the client that in order for this pillar to pull its weight, they would only need to separate thirty to forty private sales from the 600 or so that the client connected with.

The remaining 80 percent of for-sale-by-owners, who aren't hardened against Realtors, is a very big group and they will all let you in. That means eight to ten times per week you are going to be visiting and maybe presenting to a private sale, which will also bring a lot of preparation into the equation. With all that work, say goodbye to the work that was required to support your other two pillars. It's best to be very selective with those who you are going to court and work the other two simple plans required to support the other two pillars that make up your overall plan.

Step #3: Drop off the "How to save the commission" report

The "How to save the commission" report is at my website, robviviancoaching.com. Just click on the "scripts and forms" tab and download it. Once you have separated a private sale for courting, the first step in the courting process is to drop off the "How to save the commission" report. You simply drive to their property, knock on their door, and hope they are home. If they are not home, you would leave the report and follow up with a call. If you catch a break and they are home, you simply say:

"Hi ___. It's Bob from Go Get 'Em Real Estate. We spoke yesterday and you mentioned that you would be putting your home on MLS in about thirty days if you were unsuccessful in selling it yourself.

"I was just in the neighbourhood helping someone else get from house A to house B and I was going right by your door. So I thought I would give your door a rap and give you this report—"How to save the commission". That is what you are trying to do, right?"

"Oh, thank you," will always be their response.

"No problem. If you pay attention to those points, you might not have to interview Realtors in thirty days."

"Thanks again," will be their response.

"Do you mind if I ask a favour?"

"Of course."

"When you interview Realtors, can I be interviewed?"

"Oh, that would be fine."

If you really think about it, it's kind of hard for them to say no to interviewing you. The only time they say no is when they already have someone and that situation is absolute. That's okay—thank them for their time, wish them luck, and move along. After all, you already know that only one in four will work out so they just jumped into the three out of four that are not going to work for you. At least you know early, which is better than putting them on some sort of action plan. If you have no chance at a lead, it's best to eliminate it early.

If they don't have someone in mind, you have just started the process of proper courting.

Step #4: Court correctly

When a private sale says that they're going to list their home on MLS in thirty days, in most cases they list the property sooner, but it's not the day you speak to them. As previously mentioned, these folks were my third pillar and I acknowledge that almost every time a private sale indicates they would be listing in thirty days, they almost always list a week or two early.

It's a mistake for the Realtor to go today and try to retain the listing. That's the opposite of courting—that's trying to get something to happen on day one. Your success with this pillar will be in lead follow up ("courting"). Many Realtors will call private sales and take a run at them, but few will follow through and court correctly. Lead follow up begins with dropping off the "How to save the commission" report, which is essential to your success.

Courting is really not that complicated. If you separate forty to sixty over the course of the year and follow this very simple lead follow up plan, "courting", simply drop off the "How to save the commission" report, and call them every Monday and check in with how they are doing. That forty to sixty private sales will equate to ten to fifteen annual sales, which is a perfect pillar. You might underestimate how much they are going to appreciate the report and your diligence in making that weekly contact.

PILLAR #4: EXPIRED LISTINGS

The pillar of expired listings ("previously listed properties") is in many ways the easiest of all the pillars to work. Unfortunately, on many Real Estate boards, the contacting of a property after the listing has expired is strictly prohibited. However, if your Real Estate board does in fact permit you to contact an owner either on the phone or at the door after the property was unsuccessful in the sales process, and the listing agreement has in fact expired, this group is very easy to work. Think about it: there really are just two options when you call. They either want to put the property back on the market or they don't. There really isn't a third option.

If they do want to reintroduce the property back to the market again, there are just two options: they either want to relist the property with the previous Realtor or they want to interview new Realtors. So, if you are permitted to contact expired listings and you choose them as one of your three pillars, then your job here is quite basic. Contact them and find out if they want to reintroduce their property to the market and if their answer is yes, then ask if they plan to reuse the previous Realtor or interview others. If they are planning to reintroduce the property to the market and want to use a new Realtor with a different approach, suggest, "If you would give me twenty to thirty minutes of your time, then I might in fact be the Realtor that you're looking for." After your meeting, if they don't feel you are a match for them, then there's no harm, no foul.

The plan

Step #1: Call or door knock them ("be proactive")
Step #2: Close for an appointment
Step #3: Get the contract signed

You might notice that this plan only has three points. It's been my observation that in most market places this is a highly worked "pillar". In truth, there are a lot of Realtors that will call expired listings, so many that a lead follow up program here is mostly a waste of time. I have also observed that a lot of Realtors, who are willing to work for a commission quite a bit less than the industry standard, tend to work this pillar. With that in mind, you need to get them listed quickly or move along. Once a few weeks have passed, even if they do call you, they will probably say that they would like to list with you but another Realtor is willing to do it for a reduced commission. So, if you would match that reduced commission, then you can be their new Realtor. The problem is the fee that the other Realtor is willing to work for is far below your personal standard, in which case you thank them for their time and pass on the opportunity.

With expired listings, the trick is to get them under contract before all the Realtors who are willing to work for nothing get a chance to connect with them, hence the lack of lead follow up in the plan.

Step #1: Call or door knock them ("be proactive")

You need to give some serious thought to getting them under contract before they can talk to all your competition, who will probably say something that will ultimately be bad for you. You need to call them right away, first thing in the morning, and if they are not home you need to swing by their home and give the door a rap. It's important that you have a conversation with them on the first day that the property is no longer on the market. A passive approach here would definitely not work. You can't send them a letter in which you follow up a few days later. By that time, they have already talked to your competition, who have already said a few things that are not going to be beneficial to you. This pillar demands a proactive approach. If this makes you uncomfortable, then don't choose expired listings as one of your three pillars.

Step #2: Close for an appointment

It's important that while at the door or on the phone you secure an appointment. Again, you need to get this solved very quickly. Lead follow up is of very little help here. It's important that you secure an appointment prior to your competition speaking to these particular people. As previously mentioned, the conversation with an expired listing can only go one of two directions: they either want to put it back on the market, or their situation has changed and a move is no longer in their immediate plans. It's possible that if they still do wish to sell their home and relocate, they might say that they want to give it a rest for a bit. In this case, they are in scenario number one, still wanting to sell. You just need to get over the objection of "We want to give a rest for about a month or so."

Let's take a look at what to say when you contact them.

"Hi, is this ___?"

"Hi, ___, it's Bob from Go Get 'Em Realty. Did I catch you at a good time?"

"The reason for my call is that I noticed that your house is no longer on the market. Can I ask if you're planning to reintroduce your house to the market?"

At this point it's either "Yes," or "No, our plans have changed." If their plans have changed, thank them for their time and move along. If they are planning to reintroduce their home to the market, continue.

"Can I ask, when you reintroduce your house to the market would you be using the same Realtor or interviewing others?"

If they say, "We would be using the same Realtor," say this:

"If you are planning to give your previous Realtor a second chance, could I suggest maybe a quick second opinion?"

If they are open to that, great, but if not, move along. If they say, "We are planning to interview new Realtors," say this:

"Okay, if you could give me twenty to thirty minutes of your time, I would love to show you what I do to get properties sold quickly, usually over the MLS average. As a matter of fact, you just tell me when you have twenty to thirty minutes and I will change my schedule to suit you."

Remember you must book an appointment on your first call, so if you have to change your schedule, so be it. If they say, "We are going to put the property back on the market but we want to give a it rest for a couple of weeks, maybe a month," then remember that this waiting time will definitely work out badly for you, and that this is a highly worked category. Say this:

"Okay, so moving is still the plan, but you just want to give it a rest for a bit. Is that correct?"

"Yes."

"Okay, can I ask you a question?"

"Yes."

"If I had the perfect Buyer for you who wanted to make the perfect offer to you in the next thirty days during your rest period, would you look at it?"

The answer is almost always "yes" to this question.

"I haven't seen your home, so if you could fit me in for twenty to thirty minutes, whenever you are available, I would adjust my schedule to fit and I would let you know after I see your home if I think that in fact I could sell your home in the next thirty days. After we meet, if I don't think I could sell your home in thirty days, no problem, then I will be square with you, and you can have that rest time. So, if you could fit me in, when would that be?"

Step #3: Close for the signature

This step sounds basic but remember you are not the only Realtor vying for this opportunity. Once you meet with the property owner who has just completed their previous listing's contract commitment and is available to select a new Realtor, it's important that you get the contract signed while you are there. Time is of the essence. If you leave without the contract signed, the opportunity has probably passed. There is no doubt that periodically you will list previously listed properties through lead follow up, but in most cases you need to strike while the iron is hot, so take advantage of that opportunity in your initial visit. I realize and understand that most Realtors do not want to be this aggressive. If this is the case for you, then don't select expired listings (previously listed properties) as a pillar. If you connect with this plan then by all means get yourself in front of some folks that need to relist their property and do your best to not leave without the contract signed.

Lastly, many Real Estate boards have very strict rules in connection to expired listings. Please adhere to whatever rules apply.

PILLAR #5: OPEN HOUSES

This pillar is probably the most traditional of all the pillars. Realtors have been holding properties open for probably close to 100 years. Hundreds of our clients work open houses as a second or third pillar with past clients and centre of influence as their main pillar. If you choose this pillar, we require thirty open houses annually. Most of our clients load up open houses in the spring market, lay off them in the summer, and load up again in the fall. It's not that open houses are not effective in the summer, of course they are, but our clients just don't want to be there on a beautiful day. They would rather be doing something else, something non-Real-Estate, on a gorgeous summer day.

Thirty open houses do not occupy thirty weekends. Most of our clients hold properties open Saturday and Sunday on the same weekend in non-summer months. I would say that this activity for most of our clients accounts for twenty to twenty-five weekends.

The plan

Step #1: Choose high-traffic neighbourhoods
Step #2: Make the activity 12:00 p.m. – 4:00 p.m.
Step #3: Don't ask if they are working with a Realtor when they arrive
Step #4: Don't ask for personal information when they sign in
Step #5: Follow up the same day or the next

Step #1: Choose high-traffic neighbourhoods

Although it is true that periodically people will buy the open house that they view, the truth is the more common benefit for the Realtor is the opportunity to meet new potential clients. Most Realtors would be ecstatic if they sold twenty-five to forty homes annually, which means that this activity would be required to be responsible for six to ten annual transactions. If each of your three pillars kicked in six to ten annual transactions combined with six to ten random annual deals, combined together that's twenty-five to forty total transactions.

With this in mind, it's always a good idea to select a property that is located in a high-traffic neighbourhood. The more people visiting, the greater the odds of connecting with a new potential lead. It's good to keep a keen eye on what you are trying to accomplish. Remember, open houses are just one of your three pillars. If you're able to generate six to ten annual transactions from them, then you're on your way to achieving twenty-five to forty total transactions annually.

Step #2: Make the activity 12:00 p.m. – 4:00 p.m.

Traditionally, open houses have been held open Saturdays and Sundays 2:00 p.m. – 4:00 p.m. Although that is the time we do teach to hold the property open, we advise Realtors to conduct this activity from 12:00 p.m. – 4:00 p.m. I recommend that you go to the property at 12:00 p.m. to set up all your signs, turn on the music and lights, lock the door, and put a note on the door that you are working in the neighbourhood and will be back at 2:00 p.m. If you advertise your open houses in the newspaper or on MLS, advertise them for 2:00 p.m. – 4:00 p.m.

Spend the two hours between 12:00 p.m. and 2:00 p.m. door knocking and talking to the neighbours. This would be your lead-generating activity in this particular pillar. The script here is quite simple:

"Good day, folks, my name is Bob from Go Get 'Em Realty. How are you doing today?"

"I am holding the property down the street open from two until four this afternoon and I was wondering if you might know someone who is looking to move into your neighbourhood?"

If they say yes …

"Okay, great, I'm going to be there today from two till four. Have them stop buy and take a look. If they can't make it today, here's my card. Have them give me a call."

Note: don't ask for the potential Buyer's phone number at this point. They have just met you so they will not be comfortable giving it to you at this point. You know where they live. You can always follow up in the next day or two.

If they say no, which is the most common answer …

"Okay, well, a lot of buyers are going to visit this open house and, even though they don't select it, they still have an interest in the neighbourhood. So, if you had a Buyer for your home, would you consider selling?"

Our coaching clients tell me all the time that they acquire slightly more annual leads from the door knocking during 12:00 p.m. – 2:00 p.m. than from the actual open house at 2:00 p.m. – 4:00 p.m. Although a hundred or more may visit the combined thirty open houses, they are not necessarily leads just because they stopped by. The door knocking during 12:00 p.m. – 2:00 p.m. is the prospecting lead generation connected to this pillar.

Step #3: Don't ask if they are working with a Realtor when they arrive

The other day at a seminar, a Realtor made the statement that everyone who comes to her open house already has a Realtor. I hear that all the time. Of course that's not possible. The question is, why would someone say they have a Realtor? Why would an upright honest citizen tell an outright lie to a Realtor?

In order to understand this, we need to understand a little about human behaviour. A common characteristic is for everyone to defend themselves, even when no one is attacking. This characteristic puts people on guard, even when being on guard is unnecessary. Obviously when a nice young couple walk in the front door of the open house, there is no danger. You are a professional Realtor with lots of integrity. You would never say or do anything contrary to the clients' best interests. However, this young couple isn't aware of your professionalism quite yet. Right now, they feel the need to be in control of the situation. It takes a few minutes to break down this mental obstacle and for your new potential prospect to adjust and achieve a comfort level with you.

Think about it. A couple enters the front door and they're defensive. The Realtor then greets them and says, "Can I ask, are you working with a Realtor?" While the potential prospect is in the state of mind of defending from no one who is attacking, what choice do they have but to say, "Yes, we are working with a Realtor?" If they in fact are working with a Realtor, they will say "Yes, we have a Realtor that we are working with." If they currently do not have a connection with a Realtor they will still answer your question in the affirmative, "Yes, we are working with a Realtor." It's true that this honest upright couple just told a blatant lie, but it's not their fault, it's yours. You asked a direct question to someone who is in a temporary protective state of mind and they told a lie to protect their position.

Once you understand this human behaviour characteristic, the solution is simple. Greet them, establish some rapport, and once the "defending from no one who is attacking" mindset has melted away, ask them if they have a Realtor assisting them in locating the perfect home. This is where you will get the honest answer. If they are currently connected with another Realtor they will tell you. If not, they will let you know that they are available.

I have Realtors tell me, "I don't want to waste my time, so I just ask if they have a Realtor as soon as they enter the open house." There are several problems with that mindset. Firstly, it's a bad attitude, and secondly, it shows a clear lack of understanding and skill.

You might have noticed that the words I chose above were not "Are you working with a Realtor?" These words push people away from you. I chose the words, "Do you have a Realtor assisting you in locating the perfect home?" This choice of words draws people to you.

Step #4: Do not ask for personal information when they sign in

Just like the previous point, this is driven by "everyone is defending from no one who is attacking". Realtors say to me all the time that no one enters their correct phone number anymore. Think about it: they arrive at your open house with the mindset "everyone is defending from no one who is attacking," so they're currently in control of the situation for the next three to five minutes. During that time you are asking them to sign in with their name, phone number, email, identification, and "please check if you would like to receive my newsletter".

You have to understand how difficult this is for them, especially while they are in the state of mind of "defending from no one who is attacking". During this challenging process, the odds of them signing in correctly with the right name and phone number are unlikely. If you have been selling for a while, you know that traditionally about 80 percent of those visiting an open house would enter their correct name and number.

Back in the day, Realtors were not looking for more than their name and phone number, which is easy for someone to commit to, even though while they are signing the registration sheet, they are mentally "defending from no one who is attacking". Submitting their name and number is comfortable for them. It's all the additional information that puts them over the top. Different boards require certain information, so don't add to it. You are making it difficult for them.

The overall thought here is that if you would like everyone who attends your open house to sign in with their correct name and phone number, stop asking for so much and making it more difficult for them.

Step #5: Follow up the same day or the next

When prospects visit open houses, the astute Realtor understands that they are not necessarily the only open house that the prospective Buyer or Seller has visited that day. It's important that we connect with them as soon as possible to determine if in fact they are a prospective lead for us. I would highly recommend that you call them the evening on the same day you met them. If that is not possible, then the next day would be the day.

Script

"Hi, is this ___? Hi, ___, it's Bob. How are you?"

"I met you earlier today or yesterday at the open house on ___. I was wondering, did you find the home of your dreams today (or yesterday)?"

They will most likely say, "No."

"Do you mind if I ask you a few questions?"

1) "What exactly are you looking for?"
2) "If you could pick your perfect closing date, when would that be?"
3) "Can I ask your reason for moving and the attraction to that area?"

"You mentioned at the open house that you did not have a Realtor assisting you in finding the perfect home. Could I set up a few homes to show you?"

The longer you wait to call them, the greater the odds that they will be working with someone else.

PILLAR #6: CALLING AROUND JUST LISTED OR JUST SOLD PROPERTIES

When Realtors use the term "cold calling", this is the pillar or activity that they are usually referring to. Our company does not teach cold calling. We simply want every client to select three pillars and make calls or door knocking in the pillars that they choose. Choosing a random street and calling or door knocking that street would be cold calling, which is why we don't teach that. We have a much more economical and predictable tactic.

Let's start with the "just listed" side of the equation. When I teach this in a seminar format, I start by asking the audience, "Have you ever noticed when you take a listing, within seven to ten days another pops up on the street?" They respond, "That's true." Well, there is a reason for that. It's not that a neighbour notices the sign and thinks, *Hey, we should make a life-changing decision as well*; obviously that's not what happens. So why is it that this seems to happen every time? The answer lies in understanding that our planet doesn't have a procrastination problem, we have a procrastination epidemic—that's right—an all-out epidemic. That means that for the next listing you take, as soon as the sign goes up, the neighbour who needs to list their home but is currently engulfed in procrastination will be prompted out of procrastination and also put their home on the market.

If we know this will happen, we should call or door knock the neighbourhood to see if we can stumble onto this person before they call someone else. Let me explain it this way: let's pretend you and I are fishing at my lake. We are not catching anything—no bites at all—then we drift by an island and you catch a fish. You don't have to be a fisherman or fisherwoman to know it would be a good idea to poke around that island before we move along. This is a fishing metaphor for exactly what happens. When you take your listing, you should poke around the street and find the fish. In fact, now that you have read this chapter, if you don't follow this instruction on your next listing you will be disappointed with yourself when that second listing pops up seven to ten days later.

It's a good idea to call or door knock the neighbourhood a couple of days after the sign goes up. Give the local residents a few days to notice the sign and then get searching for the fish. When I was a new Realtor, my first listing was so exciting. About a week later, another listed home popped up down the street. I mentioned it to another Realtor in my office. He responded, "Yes, that happens every time." I clearly remember thinking, *Why didn't anyone tell me that?* I would have invested the time and talked to those who lived on the street. So, from that point forward, every listing I took, I went out and found the fish. Here's the thing, Realtor, you will find the fish every time. It won't always be available to you but you will find it. Sometimes when you happen upon the local resident that needs to sell and is currently procrastinating, it's there for you, and there you go, a second listing secured. Sometimes they say, "We are going to sell but we already have a Realtor." That's okay—at least you found the fish. You still did your job. At least you know.

At the door or on the phone, use this script. The door is better, but the phone will work too. Realtors always ask me about the no-call list. Most of the pillars we teach are more effective at the door, so if you are concerned about the no-call list, then get out of your office and go meet the people. It's the no-call list, not the no-contact list.

"Hi, is this ___? Hi, it's Bob from Go Get 'Em Realty. How are you doing today?"

"The reason I stopped by is I have a home for sale on your street—did you notice number ___?"

"There are going to be a lot of buyers looking at this home, and for whatever reason, they won't choose it. So if you had a buyer for your home, would you consider selling?"

As you can see, it's a pretty easy script to deliver, and very similar to the one above for the door knocking in the open houses pillar. Just keep the fishing metaphor in your mind. Trust me, there is another fish in the neighbourhood looking to get caught. It might as well be by you. So the "just listed" side of the just listed and sold pillar is quite simple: take a listing and go find the fish.

The "just sold" side is a little different. On the "just listed" side you call or door knock around your personal listings taken and "find the fish". The "just sold" property can be other Realtors' listings and other Brokers' listings, which are not necessarily yours.

If a Realtor selects a street to call or door knock in the hopes of finding someone who is thinking about moving in the upcoming future, it's usually about 100 conversations: ninety-nine "No, but thanks for calling," or "Thanks for stopping by," and one "Yes, we have been considering a move." As you know, if you have invested some time in lead generation, it's not always as cordial but it's still a "no". We teach a technique that will bring that number a lot lower, depending on the type of home and neighbourhood, between thirty to forty conversations for a "yes", which is dramatically better than the one in 100, which is typically the average.

The secret lies in calling or door knocking streets where a property has come on the market and sold very quickly. When this is the case, the Realtor's hit ratio is much higher, more like one in thirty to forty conversations versus one in 100 conversations. That's a lot less "No, but thanks for calling" or some other form of conversation that isn't quite as friendly.

It works like this: when a home comes on the market, the neighbours notice the new listing. If a "sold" sign accompanies the "for sale" sign within seven to ten days, they also notice that. When this happens, which is not that uncommon, it creates a bit of a *buzz* in the neighbourhood because of the quick sale. As local residents interact with each other, they will probably say, "Did you notice how quick number 47 Main Street sold?" The response is usually, "Yes." When a home is listed for sale and sold within seven to ten days, it creates a *buzz* on the street for about a week. If a Realtor was to call or door knock this particular street during that week when the *buzz* is in effect, their hit ratio would be between thirty to forty conversations for a "Yes, we are thinking about moving" versus the typical one in 100 conversations.

When a Realtor works a street by either the phone or at the door, if they select a street that currently does not have the *buzz*, then it would be the Realtor's conversation trying to create a buzz. They do this by telling the homeowners that the market is good and that they could achieve a good price for their home, all the while the person on the other end of the line currently has zero interest in the Real Estate market and will probably cut the Realtor's script short with a resounding "No, thanks, not interested in selling."

On the other hand, if the Realtor takes a few minutes with their MLS software and looks for streets where a home was introduced to the market and sold within seven to ten days, the Realtor can be assured that the local residents noticed and are probably talking to each other about it. Now when the Realtor calls or door knocks the street the reception will be dramatically different. When the Realtor says, "Hi, is this Mr. Smith?" they respond, "Yes."

"Hi, Mr. Smith, it's Bob from Go Get 'Em Realty."

"Yeah, Real Estate. Houses are really selling fast in the neighbourhood."

"Yes," you respond, "that's why I'm calling."

This is much better than Mr. Smith cutting your script short with an "I'm not interested" comment.

If the *buzz* already exists, they will be much more open to talk to you, which will make your lead generation a much more enjoyable process. If the majority of your prospecting calls ended with "No, but thanks for calling," Realtors wouldn't dislike prospecting so much. It's the continual cutting you off with the not-interested comment that affects Realtors. On top of the much smoother conversation as an added benefit, the hit ratio also drops from the average one in 100 to a much more efficient one in thirty to forty cordial conversations.

When calling where the *buzz* is, use the following script:

"Hi, is this ___? Hi, ___, it's Bob from Go Get 'Em Realty. How are you today?"

"You may have noticed that homes are selling very fast in your neighbourhood. Did you notice number ___?"

"A lot of buyers wanted to get into that one but did not get in in time, so if you have a Buyer, would you consider selling?"

This is a very simple script to deliver if you combine the simplicity of the script with the fact that Real Estate is already on their mind due to the property down the street selling within the first seven to ten days. The fact that the *buzz* already exists prior to your call means your script is not responsible for the creation of the *buzz*. This scenario creates a win-win for the Realtor. Real Estate is already on their mind and because this *buzz* exists already, the yeses come a lot more frequently.

Something you need to know about this process is that the buzz only lasts for about a week. So, if this is one of your pillars, then Sunday night you need to log into your MLS system and ask which properties came on the market and have sold in the first seven to ten days. The system will respond with properties that have come on the market and sold in ten days or less. Your job is to decide which of these properties you will call or door knock this week and use the simple script I provided you.

It's common for clients to ask me, "If the MLS system pulls up multiple properties, which should I choose?" That's actually a really good question. Certain types of homes and locations can have higher or lower turnover rates. You might as well work the street either by phone or at the door where your odds are higher.

Townhomes always have the highest turnover rate, usually around 8 percent or sometimes higher. For example, if a townhome complex has 100 units and 8-percent turnover, that would mean that every year eight units change hands. On the other side of the scale, older mature neighbourhoods tend to turn over at a much lower rate, usually 2 percent to 3 percent annually. So, when your MLS system supplies the list of properties that currently have the *buzz* and will continue to have the *buzz* this week, if there are townhomes on the list, select them. You might as well play the odds. It's important to note that the list supplied Sunday night is only good for this week. If this is one of your pillars, simply ask your MLS system for a new list next Sunday night—it only takes a few minutes. This pillar is more effective at the door versus the phone. It works on the phone, just better at the door.

IN A NUTSHELL

You shouldn't have all your eggs in one basket. Make sure you are actively working three different lead sources (pillars) with your past clients and centre of influence being your number one pillar. The number of Realtors we coach that are having the career they want and are ignoring their past clients and centre of influence is zero. Don't make that mistake.

*The only proper way to
eliminate bad habits is to replace
them with good ones!*

Jerome Hines

FOUR

The Magic Formula: Step Three "Lead Follow Up"

AS TIME GOES by, some things remain the same and some things change. In Real Estate, lead follow up is one of the things that has changed. In the mid 1990s, I used to teach to generate leads and keep them. I taught what is generally known as a drip program: get leads and set up a program or structure to stay in touch with them every month or two—"drip on them". This was Real Estate sales training 101. Everyone taught this process for lead follow up. The truth is, Realtors were taught for almost 100 years to secure leads and call them periodically, "drip on them". Although this process was correct at the time, it clearly is not the correct action in today's market and will never be correct again. If we don't change how we go about lead follow up, it is going to be difficult to keep up in an ever-changing Real Estate market.

The other day I was teaching a seminar at a very traditional Real Estate office. Most of the Realtors present had been selling Real Estate for many years. It was interesting to hear them tell me that they used to sell so many more homes than they do now, and that they think the market has changed. They are right—some things have changed, and how they approach lead follow up is one of the items that is no longer the way it was. But, when things changed, they did not know why that process that worked so well before didn't seem to have the same result. Realtors that have been selling Real Estate for a long period of time need to challenge some of their processes that are not working anymore and make some adjustments. So, the question you should be asking is, "What happened? Why is it that process that worked so well for almost 100 years now seems to be dramatically ineffective?"

The answer lies in the lead's access to information. Imagine I have fifteen sheep beside me. Sheep have the distinction of being the easiest creature to lead. If I grabbed one of the sheep by the collar and started to walk to my left as I said to the other sheep, "Come on, let's go, we are going in this direction," most of the sheep would naturally follow—it's sheep nature. There would be a few sheep that would not obey. They might think, *That's okay, I'm good here.* That's why we have the "black sheep of the family" saying. However, most of the sheep would just follow.

Now, in your mind's eye, imagine I have fifteen cats beside me. I pick up one and start walking to my left. I call to the other cats, "Let's go, we are going in this direction." The cats would be jumping all over and probably none of them would behave. Your leads used to be sheep, but now they are cats. You can manage sheep but you cannot manage cats. You should stop trying. It's just frustrating for you and your production is going down.

So, why the switch? Why were they sheep for almost 100 years and all of a sudden they became cats? The answer lies in understanding that they always wanted to be cats but, because of the lack of access to MLS information, they resigned themselves to being sheep. They wanted to be more independent but unfortunately they were stuck relying on whatever information the Realtor gave them every month or whenever the Realtor "dripped" on them. Then all of a sudden the MLS system showed up on the Internet. Shortly thereafter, all the Real Estate television shows started up, giving them even more understanding about the Real Estate market and how it works.

Up until this point they were reliant upon Realtors for Real Estate information—wannabe cats operating as sheep. Now, with more information than they could ever want, they can finally be the cats they always desired to be. When they first made the switch they were house cats, then barn cats, and now they are alley cats—the progression will continue. The game changed around 2005. They will never be sheep again. It used to be a matter of finding leads ("sheep") and managing them ("drip program"), but now it's a matter of finding leads ("cats") and processing them.

So, what is the perfect lead follow up system, one that any Realtor can follow? A system that is simple yet extremely effective. A system that understands and takes into consideration that one in four leads works out and that every Realtor's leads simply need to be processed, not managed. The more you accept the fact that three out of every four leads will not work out, the better off you will be. I'm not saying that three out of every four leads select another Realtor to do business with, but it's just reality that approximately 50 percent of every Realtor's leads simply don't work out at all.

It's very common for a Realtor to get a call that sounds kind of like this:

"Hi, my name is Betty, and we got your name from Gary at church. He said you are an excellent Realtor. We are thinking of moving and would like to get together so you can help guide us through the process."

This is an excellent lead and one that you should receive on a regular basis if you are calling your past clients and centre of influence every ninety days in groups of 1/11th as previously discussed. So, you meet with Betty and her family a few days later. They have a beautiful home that will sell easily and are looking to buy a slightly larger home in the same general area. You're excited, they're excited, they are happy with your evaluation of their home, and they are interested in a couple of the listings you emailed them.

At this point, everything is going well. A week or so later, Betty informs you that after further discussion with the family they have decided to stay and put in a pool and finish the basement, generating the extra bedroom they need. If you have been selling for a while you know that this happens all the time. It might not be a pool and finished basement, but it could be that their job transfer fell through or something changed within the family unit.

So, you know that if you want to sell twenty-five homes, 100 leads would be required. About half of them simply won't happen for anyone and you will be 50/50 on the other half. Let me illustrate:

Annual transaction goal: 25

Your total leads	100
Leads where their circumstance has changed and no longer will be buying or selling	50
Leads that do buy or sell, which you are 50/50 on	50
Your total annual transactions	25

The quicker you start focusing on this plan and these numbers, the quicker you will have the career you have been searching for. One in four leads working out for you doesn't mean that three out of every four leads choose another Realtor. Approximately 50 percent of your leads generated have one of dozens of valid reasons why they are no longer in the game. They appreciate your time and will be thinking about you in the future, but as of right know you should put them to the category of three out four, not working out, and keep moving forward.

A simple lead processing system

a) **Hot leads:** These are people that will buy or sell within ten days of the day you received them as a lead. Call these leads every Monday, Wednesday, and Friday.
b) **Warm leads:** These are people that will buy or sell between eleven to ninety days from the day you received them as a lead. Call them every Monday.

Lead follow up script

"Hi, is this ___?"

"Hi, ___, it's Rob from Go Get 'Em Realty. Did I catch you at a good time?"

"I'm just doing some follow up from our previous call. The other day you mentioned that [insert their story here]. Just giving you a call to see if that's still the plan or things have changed?"

Then, if it's time to book an appointment: "Okay based on that, it's time to get together. So, what's better for you? ___ or ___?"

Or, if they're going to stay in lead follow up a while longer: "Okay, no problem. I will do my job and stay in touch. In the meantime, if you see any Real Estate ads, any Real Estate signs, or anything on the Internet, just give me a call and I will get you all the information. Thanks for your time! Have a great day."

I know this is going to sound crazy but most Realtors' lead follow up system is that they just remember their leads. When I'm teaching this topic, I ask Realtors what their system is and that's exactly what they tell me. If you are following that process, just keeping your leads in your head, that's probably just fine until your goal for annual transactions is twenty, twenty-five, or maybe thirty or more. Then, all of a sudden you'd be interacting with eighty to 120 leads or more annually. You better have a better system for processing them or things are going to get a little hectic. If you follow what I'm teaching here, simply call all your leads Monday and carry the hot ones to Wednesday and Friday. The less you carry in your head, the better.

When you process your leads in a systematic fashion you become somewhat magnetic to leads. I know this sounds a little strange to think that you could actually be magnetic to leads, but it's true. There are a lot of principles on this planet that are somewhat difficult for us to understand—things like the law of attraction. You become what you think about the power of focus and momentum. The quicker and more efficiently you process your leads, the more you invoke all of the above-mentioned mysterious principles. Of course, every coin has two sides so, in this case, the more you coddle your leads, the slower you process your leads, and the less magnetic you are to attracting leads.

Remember your leads are no longer sheep. They have been cats for quite some time. Managing sheep is easy, but cats are another tale. If you are looking for some serious frustration, then try to manage cats. On the other hand, if you are seeking a productive Real Estate career, then you don't need to be an adrenaline junky to keep up with them. Just use three pillars to find most of your leads and process them.

IN A NUTSHELL

If I could summarize everything up to this point it would go like this: one in four leads work out. It doesn't matter how long you have been a Realtor or the condition of the market. Simply find the appropriate amount of leads monthly:

Annual Transaction Goal	Monthly Leads Required
20	6
25	8
30	10
35	11
40	13
45	15
50	17

These numbers are rounded off to the closest logical number.

You have to remember that you need to find the appropriate amount of leads sufficient for your goal every month, not just some of the months. One thing that I can guarantee you for sure is that every month there will be one or two valid reasons as to why you didn't find the required leads. Whether you had to write your final exam, you had two hot buyers, or maybe a transaction didn't close. None of this matters—regardless of what's going on in your business or personal life, you need to hold the required amount of monthly leads in the highest regard. You need to find these leads every month.

Your three pillars with your past clients and centre of influence as the lead pillar will supply most of the allotted leads. Obviously some leads will find you, your pillars will fill in the gap to the required amount, and then your job is to simply call them on the appropriate days and process eighty leads into twenty transactions, or 100 leads into twenty-five transactions, and so on.

Leads don't get better with time—they're not wine!

FIVE

Lead Generation: "Prospecting"

WHEN MOST REALTORS think about prospecting, it sends paralyzing energy through their body. Because of this, most Realtors spend way too much of their financial resources to draw leads to them, but if they had some understanding and confidence, they could earn those leads basically for free. My attempt in this chapter is to do exactly that—teach you how to be a great prospector in both mentality and skills.

Some leads will find you for sure, but not the total required amount of annual leads you'll need to meet your transaction number goal, be it twenty, twenty-five, or more. So, you have two choices: invest your financial resources to find them or learn how to earn them. I would highly recommend you acquire the skills and mental make up to earn them and keep your money.

There are four things that you need to understand in order to be a great prospector:

1) You need to view prospecting correctly

The other day I was teaching at a Real Estate office and they were considering hiring my company to coach the entire office, so they were checking me out. Shortly into my talk, a hand went up and the Realtor asked, "Does your company teach cold calling?"

"No, we don't teach cold calling," was my response.

"Good," he said, "because I don't want to call anybody."

"You don't have to look very far to see that this Realtor has a problem with lead generation," I responded. "We don't teach cold calling, but I want you to select three sources, called pillars, and call or door knock in the pillars that you chose. That way, it's not random, so it's not cold calling. You are working on the pillars that you chose."

"I don't see the difference," was his response.

"Well, can I ask you a few questions?" I asked him.

"Of course," he said.

Question #1

"You have a lot of people who you know, both past clients and centre of influence, who love to talk about Real Estate. When you see them, they probably ask how the market is?"

"Yes," he concurred, "they do ask that every time they see me."

"So, since we know that they love the Real Estate topic, could you call them in an organized fashion and talk about Real Estate with them versus hoping you run into them?"

"Yes, I could do that," he agreed.

"Good, because that's what we teach in regards to prospecting the pillar of past clients and centre of influence."

Question #2

"Do you ever hold open houses?"

"Yes, quite often, actually," was his response.

"Okay, could you go over at noon instead of two p.m. and talk to the neighbours about the open house you will be holding between two and four p.m. to see if they know anyone who maybe looking to move into the neighbourhood—maybe give them a chance to pick their new neighbour?"

"Yes, that does sound like something I could actually do. On a nice day, that might be kind of fun."

"Good, because that's what we teach in regards to prospecting the pillar of open houses."

Question #3

"Do you have a geographical farm?"

"No, but I was thinking about starting one."

"Okay, so once you select the proper neighbourhood that processes the proper turnover rate of 6 percent or better, would you be comfortable once they start to recognize you as the neighbourhood specialist to go on a nice day, knock their door, and have a little face to face chat with the local residents that are beginning to recognize your name?"

"Yes, that sounds kind of like door knocking around my upcoming open houses so, yes, I could do that."

"Good, because that is exactly what we teach in regards to prospecting the pillar of geographical farming."

Question #4

"There are probably a lot of for-sale-by-owners in your area who will most likely hire a Realtor to represent them at some point. Would you be comfortable calling or stopping by at their door and talking to three every day on work days?"

"No, that would totally be outside of my comfort zone to do anything with a private sale."

"No problem."

Question #5

"On every Real Estate board, there are lots of homes that came on the market and did not sell. These are 'expired listings', and they will probably reintroduce the property to the market with another Realtor. Would you be comfortable to call or stop by and see if they have interest in relisting?"

"My interest level and confidence is even lower here than with private sales," he said.

"No problem."

Question #6

"When you introduce a property to the market or a listing of yours sells, then it creates some interest on the street. Would you be comfortable calling or door knocking to try and find the people who are interested?"

"I could do that, but my comfort level is higher with my past clients and centre of influence, open houses, and geographical farming."

"Well, I guess those are your three pillars."

"I guess they are," he responded.

Cold calling is by far the worst way a Realtor can view the activity of lead generation. In fact, all that really happens is a Realtor selects the three pillars that suit them best with their past clients and centre of influence as the lead pillar.

Most Realtors' prospecting situations go like this: they go to their company convention and listen to a motivational speaker spreading the word that we should be our best and make our mark while we have a chance. The Realtor gets extremely motivated, comes back to their town, and prospects for two or three weeks then stops for about a year until this process happens again. The reason is the prospecting is random. There is a dramatic difference between random prospecting—"cold calling"—and working in the pillars that you chose—"milling around your selected pillars". When I share this illustration in a seminar format, the experienced Realtors laugh because they know this is exactly the way it goes. No one will stick to random "cold calling" for very long. The only prospecting a Realtor will commit to for the big picture is "milling around" in the pillars that they chose. FYI, I'm not knocking the motivational speaker—that's me on many occasions. He or she is doing their job correctly. The onus is on the Realtor to make the jump from cold calling to milling around in the pillars that they chose.

2) You need to be proficient on the phone and at the door

It's very common for Realtors to say to me that they are comfortable with door knocking but not the phone. It's equally as common for Realtors to tell me the opposite, too. It's okay to prefer one to the other; however, the goal is to be proficient in both activities. Personally, I prefer door knocking. I like the direct interaction at the door, but I would be limiting my ability if I fostered the mindset that I'm good with door knocking but not the phone. It's okay that I prefer door knocking in the pillars that I choose, but for me it's even better to be proficient at both door and phoning.

Some of the pillars set up better for the door and some set up better for on the phone.

Let's take a look:

1. Past clients and centre of influence: better on the phone
2. Geographical farming: better at the door—you can call, but the door is better

3. For-sale-by-owners: phone and door are equally effective
4. Previously listed properties ("expired listings"): phone and door are equally effective
5. Open house (during the two hours of prospecting prior to the open house): the door is better
6. "Just listed" and "just sold" properties: you can phone, but the door would be better

Just a side note here: with the no call list in play in both Canada and the United States, you can easily select pillars that set up better for door knocking and take the no-call list out of the equation. There is only one pillar that in the big picture is better on the phone and that is your past clients and centre of influence. Realtors often ask me if it's okay to door knock their past clients and centre of influence. Yes, but most Realtors have several hundred people in their database and, although you could door knock some of them, the only efficient way to connect every ninety days with your database would be on the phone.

If you find yourself identifying with one of the two groups—either loving the door and not the phone or vice versa—here is a perfect *affirmation* for you to say that will sort out your head and allow you to be a master of both:

"I love prospecting and I am proficient at the door and on the phone."

3) Make your prospecting contacts Monday to Friday 9:00 a.m. – 11:00 a.m.

I know what you are thinking: *Monday to Friday mornings, 9:00 to 11:00? No one is at home—most people are at work.* I know you are thinking this because it's what every new client says when they join our program and what most Realtors say to me at my seminars. I always respond with, "How do you know no one is home?

You haven't tried prospecting Monday to Friday from nine a.m. to eleven a.m."

"How do you know I haven't tried it?" is usually the quick response.

I counter with, "Because if you had tried it, you would know that lots of people are home."

Then comes the admission, "You're right. I have never tried prospecting during the week during the morning."

There are several reasons why this is the correct slot for lead generation. In fact, it is the only slot that will work long term.

a) Lots of people home

Statistically, only slightly more people are home in the evening. Families are so busy these days. When I was a kid, you had to decide which sport you wanted to play. This day and age, kids are in everything, be it dance, piano, baseball, hockey, or any number of other activities keeping parents out in the evening.

b) Nobody is having a bad day

If you want to have a real difficult time with your prospecting, make your calls in the evening. Imagine a lady commutes to work—lots of traffic, boss is difficult, commutes home, and lots of traffic again. She walks in the kitchen, sees the sink full of dishes, and as she is thinking, *Really, I'm the only one that can put those dishes in the dishwasher*, you call—that's going to go over really well. In the morning, people are much happier.

c) Your energy level is at its highest

In the morning, you have the most energy you are going to have all day. It's best to make your calls while your energy is still with you. Trust me, you can schedule prospecting for later in the day or the evening in your schedule, but when the time comes you will most likely skip it. Do it in the morning and get it done.

d) Your Real Estate distractions are at their lowest

You could have sold a house last night and be in Sign Back on another. You don't have to do anything with those situations first thing in the morning. You can let your office know about the sale and hand the offer in after 11:00 a.m. As for the offer in Sign Back, I'm sure the other Realtor isn't calling you first thing in the morning. Make your calls, hand in the offer, and call the other realtor and let them know how you are going to proceed with the Sign Back. Occasionally, Buyers and Sellers want to see you in the morning during the week, but that's rare, so use your morning more wisely and generate some leads from your pillars.

e) This is the only slot that will work

At seminars, when I ask who in the room has been selling for more than three years, lots of hands go up.

"Okay, be honest with me. The truth is, if you don't make your calls Monday to Friday 9:00 a.m. – 11:00 a.m. they are simply not going to happen."

Unanimously, they all say that's true. If it's going to get done on a regular basis, that's when it's going to happen. I know you can make the odd afternoon or Saturday morning, but we teach in our program eight weeks vacation. That's forty-four weeks of work—220 workdays per year. There is no way you are going to commit 220 afternoons to lead generation. Monday to Friday, 9:00 a.m. to 11:00 a.m. is the only slot that will work.

The first three points have been about the structure of lead generation. The next two will be about skill.

4) The twelve-second rule

This is a very interesting thing to understand and will make your prospecting much more effective. It works like this: when a salesperson of any kind—in this case, a Realtor—is talking to someone they don't know, if the Realtor talks for twelve seconds in a row, the prospect is conditioned to say no, even if they are thinking about moving. I think most Realtors are aware of this principle to a certain extent in that they know they have a certain amount of time before the prospect says they're not interested so the Realtor talks faster. This makes things worse because when a salesperson is talking fast it sends a subconscious message to the prospect's brain: *be careful, fast-talking salesperson.*

The trick is to not talk for twelve seconds in a row. This principle only lasts for one minute, then no longer applies, so go out of your way to make the first minute of your prospecting calls a little more interactive.

5) The law of reciprocation

The law of reciprocation is an interesting law. We mix it into a lot of our scripts including when someone says they are thinking about moving, which is of course the reason for making prospecting calls. Let's say you are calling around one of your sold properties and someone says, "Actually, it's good you called because we have been thinking about moving."

Right now, the Realtor thinks that the right thing to say is, "Well, I can prepare a comparative market analysis (CMA) for you, come by, sit down, and go over things with you to help you make a good decision." We think this is the correct thing to say, but unfortunately that is almost impossible for the prospect to say yes to.

Think about it: we don't know these people. If we say we will do all this work for them, they would feel like they would need to reciprocate. They would feel somewhat obligated to you because you did this work for them. They of course would not say, "Unfortunately, you just activated the law of reciprocation in my brain so I can't say yes because I will feel obligated." What they would say is, "I just want the price" or "I must speak to my wife/husband." Either way, because you activated the law of reciprocation, they will work to get off the phone.

What you need to do is book the appointment and not activate the law of reciprocation. Before you start your prospecting in the pillars you have chosen, simply look at your schedule and decide where you would like to book yourself. Perhaps Thursday evening at 8:00 p.m. or Saturday at noon. When someone indicates that they are contemplating a move, just pretend you are already going to be in their neighbourhood. That way they won't feel like you are going out of your way and the law of reciprocation will not engage. It will sound like this: "Okay, so you are thinking of perhaps making a move?"

"Yes," they respond.

"Well, as it turns out, I'm going to be in your neighbourhood Thursday night wrapping up around eight and again Saturday morning wrapping up around noon, so since I'm going to be in your neighbourhood anyway, I don't mind stopping in and answering any questions."

Their mind will think, *If they are going to be in the neighbourhood anyway, we might as well meet.* The fact that you are willing to do all the work on the chance that they might choose you comes from a good quality on your part—a good characteristic, really. Unfortunately, if you say, "I am willing to do all this," you will activate the law of reciprocation and they can't say yes.

IN A NUTSHELL

Prospecting is the most misunderstood activity in the Real Estate business. We need to stop thinking about it as cold calling and start viewing the activity correctly: "I am just milling around in the pillars that I chose." If you would like to sell twenty homes, you know that eighty leads are required. Some leads will find you every year for sure, but not the full required amount, so select three pillars with your past clients and centre of influence database as number one, along with two others that suit you, and get to work.

If you don't build your dream,
someone else will hire you to
help build theirs!

SIX

The Listing Presentation

WHEN IT COMES to the listing presentation, every Realtor on the planet desires many of them. There is a saying in Real Estate: "You have to list to last." Although that might not be totally true, you can stick around the Real Estate business by way of Buyer sales. Although it would be true that if you want to have a significant career then listings are required. Another Realtor saying is "Listings are the name of the game." Either way, the point is if you have ambitions of a significant Real Estate career, the ability to list Real Estate is mandatory.

There are five things that you need to be aware of, or good at, if your desire to be a great listing Realtor can become a reality.

1) A comfortable listing presentation

At first glance, this doesn't seem to be that big of a deal, but it's the most important piece of the puzzle, which is why it's first on the discussion list. Every Realtor entering the business shares a common goal: to be a complete Realtor with a complete, well-balanced business. A good amount of listings sold annually combined with a healthy supply of Buyer-represented sales will add up to an amazing year. Maybe fifteen listings sold, fifteen Buyer-represented sales—with a combined thirty families moved from house A to house B. For most Realtors, that would add up to a very satisfying accomplishment. I know of course that many Real Estate professionals sell way more than thirty homes annually—we have hundreds within our program—but for most Realtors, thirty annual sales would be more than big. It would be life changing.

How does this connect with the need for a comfortable listing presentation? Well, here's the thing: everything that makes you nervous or uncomfortable, your inner core avoids at all cost. So, here you are, a Realtor looking to have a balanced business. Unfortunately, performing at a listing presentation makes your heart jump a bit. When I say "performing", I mean exactly that. You get a call from a potential Seller (not a "come list me"—everyone is comfortable with "come list me"). The Seller informs you that they will be interviewing three Realtors and you will be one of them. That scenario makes you nervous or a bit anxious, knowing that you will be performing to the best of your ability and outperform two others. This situation is not true for all Realtors but true for most. Those that are not connecting here, those that say, "I love this process—the going in and performing—I find it exhilarating," good for you, that's awesome, but you are in the minority. Most Realtors reading this book are wondering how I know so much about what's going on in their head.

The problem is this: if you never develop a listing presentation that you are very comfortable with delivering, your inner person will always avoid the listing presentation. Your inner person always avoids uncomfortable or awkward situations. Your outer person wants listings badly, in fact, you probably have a goal for listings taken. You need to understand that when your inner person wars with your outer person, the inside always wins.

So, here you are, a Realtor looking to sell thirty homes in a calendar year, which will require maybe thirty listing appointments, twenty listings taken, resulting in fifteen listings sold. Even though this is an organized, well thought out structure, your inner person is still uncomfortable competing at the listing presentation and will do everything in its power to avoid uncomfortable or awkward situations. Again, your inner person always wins. This scenario is called self sabotage. Your outer person wants something badly—fifteen listings sold. Unfortunately, your inner person is desperately avoiding uncomfortable and awkward scenarios. Strange as this sounds, you are actually repelling the very thing you want. It won't matter how much you desire those thirty listing appointments equating to fifteen listings sold—you won't beat the power of your inner person.

It's also interesting how the brain explains this away as it's happening. If this is you, and it probably is, your brain wouldn't say, "My inner person is uncomfortable with competing so I'm currently self sabotaging myself." I'm pretty sure those aren't going to be the words coming out of your mouth. What you will say is this: "I kind of prefer Buyer sales because I get 2.5 percent or 3 percent."

The good news is the solution for this sabotaging problem is quite simple. Learn a listing presentation that you are comfortable delivering. That way, your inner person will be excited about the process. Now, instead of self sabotage, you will invoke the law of attraction. I'm making the point that your inner person is going to win—why not learn an amazing listing presentation that your inner person is excited about and will pull you towards instead pushing you away from? The law of attraction versus self sabotage.

The next point will be exactly that—the perfect listing presentation that you will be excited to deliver at every level of your being.

2) Every Seller has six questions

Real Estate organizations and franchises have been surveying the public for more than 100 years. Most of the surveys ask: if you were to introduce your home to the market and you interviewed a Realtor, what questions would you ask them? It's interesting that on every survey I have personally compiled they have the same six questions. As years go by the questions are the same. It's also interesting that the order of the questions never changes—it always remains the same.

Every listing appointment you attend, you can be assured that they have six questions. Imagine sitting down in front of a Seller and saying, "We know that when a Seller meets with a Realtor they have six questions. Is it okay with you if we just discuss those six questions and make a decision? Can we do that?"

Trust me, I have delivered that exact statement over a thousand times and 100 percent of the time they respond with a resounding "yes". Actually, as you are aware, sometimes Realtors spend too much time at the listing presentation talking about random things. When they leave, the Sellers comment to each other, "Wow, that was two hours. I hope the Realtor tomorrow night doesn't take so long."

So when you say to them, "We know when a Seller meets with a Realtor they have six questions. Is it okay with you folks if we just discuss those six questions and make a decision? Can we do that?"

Don't be surprised if they get a little excited with their "yes, that would be great" response.

Don't say, "I guess the other Realtor was here a long time last night." You can be assured that happened. I hope that's not you taking two hours to present—after all, they only have six questions.

I would highly recommend you come up with some simple information to answer the Sellers' six questions.

1. Why should we choose you?
2. Why should we choose your company?
3. What are you going to do to get the maximum price in the shortest time frame?
4. What do you charge?
5. What is my home worth?
6. What is going on in the local market?

Obviously the odds of your local Real Estate Board calling your upcoming listing presentation and asking them to complete a short survey and them being willing is highly unlikely. However, if that was the case and the survey asked, if you were to introduce your home to the MLS system and you interviewed a Realtor, what questions would you ask them?—these six questions would definitely be their answer.

3) Sellers can't make a decision with any unanswered questions

If any of the above six questions are not answered, their brain will not be in a state to make a decision. They can only make a decision when all subconscious questions are answered.

They of course would not say, "I can't make a decision because several of my subconscious questions remain unanswered," although that is exactly what's happening. What they would say is, "Your presentation was really good but we need to think about it." Believe me, Realtor, they can't sign the contract with unanswered questions. The good news is they only have six, so it shouldn't be that difficult to answer six questions and get a decision.

4) One-step versus two-step listing appointments

A one-step listing appointment is seeing the property for the first time and presenting, which will require you to possess the skill of adjusting up or down in regards to price, depending on condition and upgrades or the lack of upgrades. A two-step listing presentation is viewing the property in advance and presenting a few days later.

At seminars, it's interesting how many Realtors have already decided which category they fall into. Realtors regularly tell me that they are a two-step or one-step Realtor, then ask me which I was. I always say I'm both—sometimes I feel I need to see the property in advance and sometimes I don't think an advance viewing would be required. Some market places have a lot of unique homes in which a two-step approach would be wise, but on the other hand some market places have a lot of generic housing styles, which would lean more towards the one-step approach.

The best approach would be to not decide to be a one-step or two-step. Just do what makes sense.

5) The close is the natural ending to an organized presentation

If that statement is true that also means that the opposite is true: the close is an awkward ending to an unorganized presentation. Both of those two statements are true, I know that. Any Realtor who sits in front of a Seller knows that when a Seller meets with a Realtor they have those six questions above.

Then simply answer all six questions in the proper order and then close for the signature—that will be the natural ending. Otherwise, if your presentation does not follow a simple logical structure and bounces all around, the close for the signature will be awkward and truthfully most Realtors will avoid the awkwardness so they will present and leave with the contract unsigned.

IN A NUTSHELL

If you don't have a listing presentation that you are very comfortable to deliver, your inner person will always avoid uncomfortable situations and you will be sabotaging your own efforts and your career. It's best to learn how to answer the Seller's six questions and then you are done. It won't matter for the rest of your career if your appointment is a $100,000 or a $1,000,000 property or a commercial building—everyone has six questions. Simply answer them and get the contract signed.

Don't be afraid to fail,
be afraid to not try!

SEVEN

Handling Objections

WHEN I'M TEACHING this topic in a seminar format, I always start with the question, "Who would like to learn some magic?" They look at me with an odd look obviously. "Okay, do you ever have Sellers who don't want to pay full commission?"

"All the time," is the quick response.

"What if I could show you a way to get them to want to pay full commission?"

"Well, that would be magical," they agree.

I inform them that that is exactly what I'm going to teach them, and I'm going to explain it to you in this chapter. To understand this magical technique, we must first explore something called the law of reciprocation. This was briefly mentioned in a previous chapter, you'll recall. The law of reciprocation is a very interesting principle and really simple to understand. The brain has a very strong desire to reciprocate. If someone agrees with you, you naturally want to reciprocate and agree. If someone disagrees with you then the reverse is true—you have a strong desire to disagree.

The law of reciprocation isn't something that you control, it's something that controls you. We have all been in a situation when we say something about a topic that we don't know much about and someone challenges us that that is not the way it works—we then reciprocate and defend our position. The truth is, we don't really know we're right. Sometimes this debate can become quite heated, so why would we vehemently defend a position when we know in our heart there is a really good chance that we are wrong? This is an example of the law of reciprocation controlling us. We are not stubborn or argumentative, actually, this debate is not our fault. It's the other person's fault—they challenged us, after all, activating the law of reciprocation.

This means the next time a client gives you an objection, if you agree with them and activate the law of reciprocation in a positive manner, their brain will have a very strong desire to agree in return. As you know, every coin has two sides, which also means that next time a Seller indicates they would like a reduced commission because the other Realtor is offering that, and you tell them through your objection handler why that is a bad idea, then you are challenging them. They will automatically challenge back. Unfortunately, you activated the law of reciprocation in a negative manner. Either way, the law of reciprocation is going to be in effect. You control if it will be positive or negative, whether they will have a strong desire to agree or disagree.

If you really think about it, the reason we call it an objection is because the client is saying something that we as Realtors don't like, be it cutting the commission, listing it high, or making a low offer, or they have a friend in the business. In all cases, we disagree with the objection handler, but we must understand that the potential client's motive is correct. If a Seller asks for a reduced commission, we as Realtors think that the reduced commission is an incorrect commission, which is fine—I personally feel we should be compensated properly for the skills we bring to the table, which is more than most Sellers understand.

However, I also acknowledge the motive of the Seller. After all, these are just hard-working folks trying to look after their hard-earned money and there is nothing wrong with that. In fact, that is a correct motive—it doesn't make the low commission correct, but the wanting to do well for themselves is fine. It's the same as a Seller wanting to price their home too high. The overpricing isn't correct, but the motive for wanting to get more is fine. If I were selling, I also would have a strong desire to do the best I can for my family.

If you look at their position honestly, you would see that their actual objection is incorrect but their motive is correct. What I'm going to show you is how to agree with their motive and activate the law of reciprocation in a positive manner so that when you are delivering your objection handler, their brain will have a very strong desire to agree with you, which will make your objection handler somewhat magical. It's important to understand that you are not being condescending or patronizing—it's easy to agree with them when you understand that their motive of wanting to do the best they can for their family is correct. We teach a very simple communication technique called Repeat, Approve, and Build a bridge. It's not magic but it's pretty close.

Repeat: Tells them that you listened and you heard. Starts with "okay" and ends with "is that correct?"

Approve: Tells them that their motive is correct.

Build a bridge: Permission to continue.

Let's take a better look at each of these three steps before we discover how the whole process sounds.

Repeat:

This step tells them that you listened and you heard. It starts with "okay" and ends with "is that correct?" At a listing presentation, a Seller says, "Would you be willing to reduce your commission?" Instead of telling them all the reasons why that is a bad idea, which would be shooting them down, which would activate the law of reciprocation in a negative manner, giving their brain a strong desire to shoot you down, and showing lack of skill on the Realtor's part—instead, you demonstrate current advanced skills by saying, **"Okay, so you are wondering if I would be willing to reduce the commission, is that correct?"** Now the Seller knows that you listened and you heard. It's very simple, just start with "okay", say what they said, and end with "is that correct?"

Approve:

Remember it's not the objection that you are approving—it's their motive. The reason we call it an objection is because we don't think it's the best plan or route for them, but their motive is correct, so stay on that. It's easy to be 100 percent sincere with them. This technique is not a magical technique to manipulate people. You are at a listing presentation with a motivated seller who is thinking about listing with a Realtor who has agreed to discount to a level well below your standard. You honestly feel that it's in the best interest of the Seller to pay you a bit more and get proper representation, so your motive is clearly in the best interests of the client. There is a lot on the line and if things don't go well they could be in trouble. Again, the best scenario for them is to pay you more and have things done correctly with a proper marketing budget. Your heart is pure, you are not looking at what's best for you—it's clearly about the client.

Please connect on the fact that your approval of their situation is 100 percent sincere on your part. You definitely agree that when folks are moving they should have a strong desire to do as well as they can for themselves. It would sound like this: **"I know you work hard for your money, and when you are moving from house A to house B you should be looking to do as well as you can. I'm not moving right now but if I was, like you I work hard for my money and I would have a strong desire to do as well as I can. So I have no problem with that."** Please make the connection that you are not patronizing them, but you fully agree with their motive of maximizing their financial position. Now that you have sincerely approved them, you have activated the law of reciprocation, giving their brain a very strong desire to reciprocate and agree with you, and the thing that you are going to be saying shortly is your objection 'handler', the reason why it's a much better idea to pay a bit more and get to house B safely and securely.

Build a bridge:

The bridge is very simple and the purpose lies in the name: build a bridge. Build a bridge from your approval over to your objection handlers, the conversation that their brain is desperately wanting to agree with. There are really only two bridges. One is you want to tell a story. It would sound like this: **"Can I share something with you?"** Or, if you want to show them something, perhaps your plan of action, the bridge would be **"Can I show you something?"** It's very simple.

The skill in handling objections isn't in your clever objection handler, it's in the ability to be a skilled Realtor and look for the motive as to why this business opportunity is giving you an objection; to look for their motive and to acknowledge that although you don't agree with their objection you certainly do see the rationale in their motive. Take the time to Repeat, Approve, and Build a bridge, and watch the law of reciprocation control them.

In our coaching company we never teach to practice your objection handlers. When you do, you will most likely throw them back at your prospect quicker in a rebuttal format. If you really think about it, you probably get three to five objections in your entire career. It can't be that difficult to think up three to five logical things to say. We do teach to our clients to practice the skill part of the objection handling process of Repeat, Approve, and Build a bridge.

If you are not sure what to say as a logical objection handler, visit our website: robviviancoaching.com.

IN A NUTSHELL

Everyone on the planet is controlled to a certain extent by the law of reciprocation. Next time you get an objection, it's best to Repeat, Approve, and Build a bridge, and place their brain in a state of having a strong desire to agree with you. Your clever objection handler works well when they have a desire to agree versus disagree.

Arguing with a fool proves
there are two!

Doris Smith

EIGHT

Managing Your Time

THERE ARE MANY helpful time management tips and techniques for business people and people in general. Although that also applies to the Realtor population, there are really three key time management principles. Any Realtor who adheres to these three principles will never have a time management challenge again ever. That would be amazing, so let's take a look at them, and the great news is they are pretty simple to implement.

Step #1: Core beliefs

I have this one first because it's the most important of the three. The other two are a structure format, something to do. This one is in the mindset category—a way to think, a way to view something. Every Realtor gets a Real Estate license for the same two reasons: to make a lot of money and to have a flexible schedule.

It's really funny when I get a chance to speak to a class of new Realtors or a group currently in the process of obtaining their licenses. I make the suggestion, "You are all in the process of becoming a Realtor for the same two reasons. Does anyone know what they are?"

Literally within seconds someone shouts out to make a lot of money followed very closely with having a flexible schedule. Correct. Those are the two reasons that all Realtors become Realtors.

1. To make a lot of money
2. To have a flexible schedule

I inform the class that unfortunately the flexible schedule is going to get in the way of all the money and is the main reason most Realtors fail. At this point I definitely have their attention.

Core beliefs are the reason why people do what they do or the reason why they believe what they believe. Core beliefs are one of the most powerful forces on the planet. Your inner person will defend your core beliefs at an extremely high level and doesn't really differentiate the importance of the core belief—just that it is a core belief and must be protected and enforced.

So, Realtors embark on a Real Estate career with the thoughts (core beliefs) of making a lot of money and having a flexible schedule. Unfortunately, the core belief of flexible schedule is the opponent of time management. It's no wonder Realtors have a challenge with time management. They endure an entire career trying to stay on schedule, the whole time their inner person is protecting the core belief of flexible schedule, which again is the opponent of time management.

At the writing of this book, I have taught thousands of seminars spanning back over twenty years. The number of Real Estate seminars that I have conducted where everyone was on time is zero. You would think that with thousands of opportunities at least once everyone would be on time.

I wish I could get rid of this core belief for you. If I could I would. As long as you hold on to this belief, time management will continue to be a challenge for you. It's really quite comical. When teaching this particular seminar, I start with the question, "Who would say that they have a time management challenge?" Every hand goes up usually accompanied with a resounding, "Oh, my gosh, you have no idea." Actually, I do have an idea. I know exactly what's happening. I am standing in front of a room full of Realtors who are subconsciously holding onto the core belief of flexible schedule which, in turn, is attacking their time management skills, the skills they possessed prior to becoming a Realtor.

Once I explain this condition they get it right away, so all we have to do is let go of the core belief of flexible schedule and we are fixed, is that correct? Yes. Can we hold onto the "make lots of money" core belief? Yes, that would be a good idea. In fact, the "make a lot of money" has a greater chance of happening without the core belief of flexible schedule hindering the process.

The truth is, Realtors selected those two core beliefs without much thought. One core belief is correct and one is incorrect. The core belief of making a lot of money is correct, not for the sake of making money—you have to want success for the right reasons; your perspective and values need to be in line. If you haven't read the book I wrote, *The Grass is Greener on This Side of the Fence*, I would recommend you do. It's an excellent book on perspective.

The core belief of flexible schedule is the one accidently and incorrectly selected and will hinder your entire growth path, so it's best to get rid of it. The good news is your inner person will only defend a belief if you keep believing it. If you were to give it a better thought, it would be more than happy to make the switch and defend the new thought with the same vigour it's currently protecting your core belief of flexible schedule.

Why not replace the core belief of flexible schedule with "I am a time management specialist". Start saying and believing this thought and not only will your time management improve but your entire Real Estate career will also follow along.

I mentioned earlier that the first of the three points is on the mindset side and the following two are practical steps. Be clear that if you don't sort out what we just talked about, the core belief part, the two practical steps will be of no benefit. They are no match for the power of your inner person protecting the core belief of flexible schedule. First things first, that's got to go. Then the next two steps will be helpful.

Step #2: To-do list

I realize this sounds pretty basic but there are a couple of things you need to know about making a to-do list.

You need to make the list the night before

The brain is an amazing thing and sometimes it appears to mess with us on purpose. Let's say it's a Tuesday night and you are thinking about all the things you need to do the next day. As an example let's pretend it's a pretty busy day. You have eight tasks that need to happen, so you organize your tomorrow as you roll them over in your head.

1. Hand in my new listing
2. Write the ad on the Smiths' house
3. Book showing for the Whites
4. Return that Internet call
5. Report to my Sellers the last week's activities
6. Pick up my lock box from Main Street
7. Follow up with a few leads
8. Call the referral I received from one of my friends

It's interesting that the night before it's easy to make this list, but in the morning you can't remember the eight items on today's to-do list. That's not just your brain—that's everyone's brain. That's what I meant by it seems that our brain messes with us just for fun. I'm sure that's not the case but it appears so. You are sitting at your desk first thing in the morning with your trusty cup of coffee, pen in hand. *Okay, I know I have eight things to do today. Alright, process this listing, book showing, write that ad … that's three, I know there's eight.* You take a sip of coffee, tap your pen on the desk, trying desperately to remember the other five. *Oh, I have to pick up the lock box, that's four.* After a few minutes you just decide to get started. You will remember the other four as the day goes by. This is exactly how everyone's brain works—crystal clear the night before and foggy in the morning.

So, if that's how it's going to go, then you better make the list the night before and work efficiently through your list the following day. What's really funny is as the day goes by you will remember most of the other tasks, but your brain usually saves one for the moment your head hits the pillow—you were supposed to call the referral from your friend. *Darn*, you think, *what time is it? Eleven-thirty, well that's too late to call.*

When I'm teaching this in a seminar format, everyone is laughing because this is exactly what happens. If you want to be good at time management, make your to-do list the night before and follow it the next day versus getting started with half a list because that's all you could remember in the morning, then scrambling all day as your brain gently reminds you of your tasks.

Step #3: First item starts at 11:00 a.m.

As mentioned in the chapter on prospecting, you would be wise to make your lead generation calls or door knocking Monday to

Friday 9:00 a.m. – 11:00 a.m. When you write your to-do list the night before, write 11:00 a.m. beside the first point—that way, in the morning when you wake up and start your morning routine, everything is organized. That first item has nothing to do with 9:00 a.m. It's scheduled for 11:00 a.m. and you are free to lead generate in the pillars that you choose to build your career on.

It's interesting when I'm teaching this in a seminar—the students usually say, "With those eight items, would I have time to commit two hours to that morning prospecting?" I respond, "That's a great question. Let's figure out how much time each of these items should take." I simply ask the group how much time each item will take and whatever time they give me I accept. Then we add it up and it never is more than four to five hours for the total list. So, if we started the first item at 11:00am, we are finished between 3:00 p.m. and 4:00 p.m. and we can go home for an early dinner.

IN A NUTSHELL

I know that there are many courses and material on the topic of time management, but believe me when I tell you that any Realtor who implements these three principles will be a time management wizard. Any Realtor who consciously lets go of the core belief of flexible schedule, makes their to-do list the night before, and starts the first item at 11:00 a.m. immediately following their daily lead generation will never have a time management problem ever again.

The bad news is time flies,
the good news is you're the pilot!

Michael Altshuler

NINE

Pre-Qualifying

PRE-QUALIFYING IS AN interesting topic and one of the most misunderstood topics. Most Realtors think that pre-qualifying their lead is how much they make, how much equity they have, what kind of job stability they have, and so on. It's true that you will require that information in order to service them correctly, but that is not pre-qualifying for the Realtor.

Pre-qualifying for the Realtor is finding out their story, where do they want to go, when do they need to be there, and why are they relocating to that particular area. If a Realtor has a desire to sell twenty-five homes in a calendar year, at this point you should be clear that they require 100 leads. That means 100 times the Realtor must pre-qualify each and every lead: where do they want to go, when do they want to be there, and why are they relocating to that particular area. After the pre-qualifying is completed and your new lead has opened up to you, you will then collect the data required to service them correctly: equity, job stability, and so on—the data that up until now you have considered to be pre-qualifying.

Of all the services a person interacts with while moving from house A to house B or just buying house A, they interact most with:

1. A Realtor
2. The bank
3. A home inspector
4. A lawyer
5. A stager

And maybe a few others. It's the Realtor who operates on a much higher level over the other services and on a much higher emotional plateau. It's important that we make the emotional connection with the clients. What could be better than your next sign call opening up to you and telling you their whole story, where they desire to move to, when they want to arrive there, and why are they relocating to that particular neighbourhood. Unfortunately, if they don't know you, they will be very uncomfortable and apprehensive to tell someone they don't know their personal story. However, you still need their story. If your goal is twenty-five annual transactions and 100 leads are required, that means 100 prospects need to confide in you and be comfortable expressing their personal story to someone they don't know. I'm sure you are a fine Realtor with a great reputation, but at this point they are a sign call or an Internet call or maybe they just walked into your open house. In the future they will discover what a fine Realtor and person you are, but they don't know that yet, and you need to pre-qualify your lead right now in the beginning of your relationship.

In psychology there is a phrase that explains a condition that effects all of us, which I mentioned earlier: "everyone is defending from no one who is attacking", which would explain a possible prospect's apprehension to opening up to a Realtor so soon.

Of course, I have a solution. There is a way to get prospects who don't know you, and are being cautious for good reason, to open up and tell you everything. The solution starts with understanding something about the brain. If you have a direct conversation with someone you don't know, which will be the majority of your leads, they will instantly defend. For example, you sell a listing and the sold sign goes up, which prompts a neighbour to call you because they also need to sell. The conversation usually goes like this:

"Hi, I noticed you sold number forty-seven. We are also thinking about selling."

"That's great! Where are you planning to move to or when would you be planning to introduce your property to the market?" This is too direct a question to someone you don't know, who is defending from no one who is attacking.

"I didn't say we were moving for sure—I just want to know the price!"

This is a pretty predictable conversation. Now the prospect is moving away from you. You do need the information where are they moving to, when do they need to be there, and why are they moving to that location. The trick is in asking the questions in a hypothetical format. When we ask hypothetical questions, their subconscious mind sends them a message that this conversation is not real, and that it's just hypothetical. In turn, because they are having a hypothetical conversation, their subconscious mind sends them a message that says, *We are in a* safe zone, *feel free to tell them everything, no danger here*, and in turn they drop the "everyone is always defending from no one who is attacking" mindset.

If you just start your questions with these five words they will tell you everything: **"If you were to move."** These five words make the conversation hypothetical and the conversation will probably go like this:

"I noticed you sold number forty-seven. We are also thinking about selling."

"Okay, *if you were to move*, where would you be planning to relocate to?" This is now a hypothetical question, which allows them to open up to you. No danger here.

"Oh, we are looking to move to Brooklyn."

"Wow, great, *if you were to move* and you could pick your perfect closing date, when would that be?"

"Well, our new home will be ready in 120 days."

"Wow, that's great! *If you were to move*, I'm a little curious, what takes you to that location?"

"Our daughter is having our first grandchild and as a sub benefit we will be forty-five minutes closer to our weekend cottage."

That is pre-qualifying your new lead. You now know that they have purchased a new home closer to their daughter and first grandchild, that they take possession in 120 days, and as a sub benefit they will be forty-five minutes closer to their weekend cottage. Now, go ahead and collect the required data necessary to service them correctly.

Every lead you acquire you need to pre-qualify on your first conversation. If you follow this process they will tell you everything. Think about how powerful your listing presentation will be now that you know their story.

Imagine sitting down in front of them and opening with their story in the beginning of your presentation. "Thanks for having me over to discuss the marketing of your home, and I hope you think I'm the right Realtor to sell your home for a lot of money and get you folks closer to your first grandchild. Congrats again! And as a sub benefit, forty-five minutes closer to the weekend getaway—I'm sure you love that."

When you are able to open your listing presentation with their story then go on to simply answer the Seller's six questions, your listing presentation will be insanely powerful.

IN A NUTSHELL

Pre-qualifying for the Realtor is finding out their story: where they want to go, when they want to be there, and why are they making a move to that location. Unfortunately, if they don't know you they will be very apprehensive to opening up to you unless you ask all the questions hypothetically. Then, their brain will send them a message that they are in a *safe zone, no danger here, feel free to open up*. It's not magic, but it's pretty close.

Assumptions are the termites of relationships!

Henry Winkler

TEN

PRICING

PRICING REAL ESTATE is an interesting topic and where most Realtors make a mistake. There are a couple of things that you need to know, and if you can master them, pricing will never be a problem for you again.

The first thing is "motivation over price". When I teach this topic everyone in the class agrees, yes, motivation over price. Then why do you push the price so aggressively at the listing presentation? If we really believe motivation over price, we would back off a little on the push for the right price. The truth is, most Realtors push so hard for the right price they push themselves out of the equation. Once they leave, the Sellers say to each other, "We are not having that person back." That Realtor might agree that motivation over price makes more sense but they operate price over motivation.

When at a listing presentation, if the Seller wants to try it high and they are motivated to sell, you would be wise to take the listing. Of course, you should try to convince the Seller that pricing the property correctly from the beginning would be a much better idea. Just don't make the mistake of pushing the price to the point where you push yourself out of the equation.

There is a balance between taking the listing too easily and pushing yourself out of the equation. In fact, if you offer to take the listing too easily, you will appear too weak and the Seller will likely take the offer off the table. On the other hand, if you push too hard you will push the Seller away from you. The perfect balance is the A, B, C, D technique. It allows you to pursue the right price but not at a level that you would be jeopardizing your opportunity to secure the listing. The A, B, C, D technique sounds like this:

"We want to try $650,000 for a couple of weeks," says the Seller.

"Okay, so you want to try $650,000 for a couple of weeks, is that correct?"

"Yes."

"Well, I know you work hard for your money and have a desire to make as much as you can, which is of course the right idea. I'm not selling myself but if I was selling, I too would have a strong desire to make as much as I can."

"Thank you."

"Do you mind if I share something with you?"

This is not the A, B, C, D technique, it's Repeat, Approve, and Build a bridge, which comes before every objection handler—in this case, the objection that we want to try it high. If you are not clear on this technique go back and reread the chapter on objection handling. The A, B, C, D technique is this:

"In every market place, a grade A Buyer comes in and takes what they perceive to be the best property. The grade A Buyer offers the right price, they close on the right date, and they don't ask for your stuff. It's perfect. Next comes the Grade B Buyer, who also pays the right price and closes on the right date, but they ask for some items, perhaps the appliances, still a good buyer. Next comes the grade C Buyer—they don't offer as much money and the closing dates don't line up. Then the grade D Buyer, which is your shrewd investor. So, Mr. Seller, if you had a choice, which would you prefer to work with—the grade A or Grade D Buyer?"

"Well, the grade A Buyer, of course," responds the Seller.

"Of course you would. I'm sorry for asking such a rhetorical question." You have to say that somewhat jokingly, because that is a rhetorical question. "Well, the active listing on the comparative market analysis is $599,000 and we are going to be $650,000. So, what price would we have to be in order for the grade A Buyer to choose us over the property listed at $599,000?"

"We would probably have to be listed at around $599,000."

"Correct. Perhaps we should introduce your property at that price and attract the next grade A Buyer."

This technique is the perfect amount of dialogue. You are not offering to take the listing too easily and appearing weak at the same time. You are not pushing too hard and pushing yourself out of the opportunity. The success rate is about 50 percent, so half the time they will abandon their desire to price it high and list with you at the correct price. What's awesome about this technique is that although it's only fifty-fifty at the listing presentation it's almost 100 percent two or three weeks later.

A few weeks later in your weekly update, you will point out that three or four similar properties have sold and the dialogue will sound like this:

"Good day, Mr. and Mrs. Seller, just wanted to give you our weekly update. We have been on the market for two weeks now. I mentioned to you last week that that new listing came up at $599,000 and it has now sold, so that's four homes similar to yours that have sold since we came on the market. Do you remember when we introduced your home to the market I mentioned the A, B, C, D Buyers?"

"Yes, I do remember that."

"Well, as you can see, that process has just taken place with the four sales going to the A, B, C, and D Buyers."

"Yes, I can see that." They are always a bit disappointed that they just missed out on the cycle.

"Would you like some great news?"

"Yes."

"The cycle happens every two or three weeks. Would you like to get involved in the next cycle?"

"Yes, I would."

The A, B, C, D technique is fifty-fifty at the listing table and almost 100 percent two or three weeks later once you have pointed out that a cycle has just happened and simply ask if they would like to get involved in the next cycle. For my entire Real Estate career I never really worried about pricing. If they wanted to price it high, I just Repeated, Approved, and Built a bridge, explained the A, B, C, D Buyers, and if they priced it right at the table, great, but if not, two or three weeks later was fine with me.

I know that you might be thinking that the A Buyer takes the best property, then the B Buyer takes the next best one, and so on—that isn't exactly how it works. Of course I know that that is why it works so well. I think most Realtors educate their clients, so that after they sell their home and sell them another, the client is so educated that they can now pass the Real Estate exam. I'm joking, but when handling an objection it's best to tell a story that is so rudimentary and basic that the clients get it. That's exactly what the A, B, C, D technique is—a basic rudimentary story that they understand.

I'm not advising that you take all listings; I'm saying motivation over price, so take all listings that are priced right, and if they want to price it high, only take the listing if they are motivated.

If they want to price it high and they are not motivated, I would highly recommend you thank them for their time and very politely leave. The good news is there is a real easy way to tell if they are motivated or not. Those who are motivated and want to try it high always say these words: "We just want to try it for a period of time"—usually two or three weeks—if you hear this dialogue, follow the process just discussed and take the listing.

If they want to price the property high and they are not motivated, they always say these words: "I want $650,000 in my pocket." Those who are motivated will never use the words *in my pocket* and those who are unmotivated will never use the words *I just want to try it for a couple of weeks.* As a rule of thumb, if you hear the words *in my pocket*, thank them for their time and very politely leave. This situation will not end well for you.

IN A NUTSHELL

In regards to pricing, don't make the mistake of pushing too hard for the right price at the listing. Simply Repeat, Approve, and Build a bridge, and explain the A, B, C, D technique. Let the chips fall where they fall. If it works at the listing presentation, that's awesome, but if not, two or three weeks later is pretty much for sure. If you hear *in my pocket*, run!

The way to get started is to quit talking and start doing!

Walt Disney

FINAL THOUGHTS

I HOPE THAT you found this book helpful. A Real Estate career is an awesome career and I hope that you take full advantage of it. It's entrepreneurship at its maximum. You can experience such an awesome life at so many different levels. You will of course experience financial benefits that quite honestly most people will never experience. You will have the satisfaction of helping others accomplish their dream of home ownership.

I hope that you understand the opportunity that you have to live in a free country and that others have fought on your behalf to allow you the freedom that you enjoy, the freedom to be an entrepreneur, and the freedom to express yourself, to move freely, and accomplish your dreams and desires. I hope you understand the magnitude of the opportunity afforded to you.

There is a saying, "If your ship doesn't come in, swim out to it." The Real Estate ship does not come in. Swimming is required. I hope you can catch a spark and allow that spark to grow into an uncontrollable fire of success and, in turn, help many people achieve their goal of home ownership and in return your dreams and aspirations will also become a reality.

Make your mark. You owe it to those who paid the ultimate price for you to have this opportunity!
Rob

No one sets a goal to be broke, out of shape, negative, and lazy—that's just what happens when you don't set goals!

MEET THE AUTHOR

Rob Vivian Coaching was founded in 2008. It is an international coaching and training company, however, we are proudly Canadian! After almost 20 years of coaching, thousands of seminars and over 75,000 coaching calls, Rob still finds immense satisfaction every time a client realizes their full potential. Rob has trained thousands of Realtors with his success proven scripts and skills strategies.

Our coaches here at Rob Vivian Coaching are current top Realtors from around North America. Rob not only speaks in Canada but is an international speaker with an extensive amount of knowledge in both the US and Canadian Real Estate Markets. We strive to provide a fun and motivational environment with a high level of accountability for our clients. Our goal is to meet the needs of every individual agent by providing several different coaching formats.

ACKNOWLEDGEMENTS

I WOULD LIKE to acknowledge the people who helped make this book a reality, starting of course with my family, Coleen, Josh, and Corissa, who all play major roles in the day-to-day operation of the company, and James, who isn't part of the family but he thinks he is.

I would also like to thank our coaches, who are amazing, and our clients, who of course without them none of this would be possible.

A special thanks goes out to Amy O'Hara for her amazing editing skills.

I want to express my gratitude to the multitude of folks who have helped me along the way—there are too many to mention, but you know who you are.